Fascinating FACTS

≥TO BLOW YOUR≤

CuriOus

≥ MIND ≤

WILD AND WACKY THINGS
YOU NEVER KNEW

Fascinating FACTS

TO BLOW YOUR Curious MIND

MJC MATTHEW

sourcebooks

Sourcebooks and the colophon are registered trademarks of Sourcebooks.

Published by Sourcebooks
P.O. Box 4410, Naperville, Illinois 60567-4410
(630) 961-3900
sourcebooks.com

Originally published in 2023 in Great Britain by Ebury Spotlight, an imprint of Ebury
Publishing. Ebury Spotlight is part of the Penguin Random House group of companies
whose addresses can be found at global.penguinrandomhouse.com

Cataloging-in-Publication Data is on file with the Library of Congress.

Printed and bound in the United States of America.
VP 10 9 8 7 6 5 4 3 2 1

This book is dedicated to my nan, who we lost to dementia.

She was not just my nan, but my best friend. Any time she would ask me about my job or talk about me to her friends she would describe me as a writer, as I would 'write' my scripts to film on TikTok and YouTube. I guess I can now finally say that my nan was right, I am now a writer.

I love and miss you so much, Nan. Thank you for everything you ever did for me! I am the man I am today thanks to your influence.

Contents

Animals

Food

Bonus facts

CHAPTER 1:

OUR WORLD

When we think about the craziest fact we know, it most likely leads us to another planet or into space itself. However, the small blue dot that we call home breeds some of the most fascinating and mind-boggling facts that I for one have ever heard of. Here are the craziest facts about our world.

General facts

Shuffling a deck of cards is deeper than you think. If you shuffle a deck of cards, it is statistically likely that you will have shuffled them into an order no pack of cards has ever been in before, and most likely never will be again. Essentially, you are the first person in history to have shuffled the cards into that exact sequence.

The Statue of Liberty used to be a different colour. The Statue of Liberty as we know it today is green. However, this is only due to the oxidation that has occurred. The statue is made of copper, so in fact it was originally the colour of a one penny coin.

All blue-eyed people are related. All blue-eyed humans share one common ancestor born 6,000–10,000 years ago. Blue eyes in humans are actually caused by a mutation in the HERC2 gene. Having this mutation is like having a genetic switch that turns off your body's ability to make brown pigment in your eyes – which leads to you having blue eyes. This all started with one human many thousands of years ago, so next time you see someone with blue eyes, say hello to your new family member.

Toilet paper was invented in the 1800s. You might want to take a minute to thank a kind gentleman by the name of Joseph Gayetty. That name might not mean a lot to you immediately, but it is thanks to this man that toilet paper was sold in shops for the first time in 1857. He called the product 'Medicated Paper for the Water-Closet'.

You might live in the country with the most tornadoes. If I asked you which country in the world has the most tornadoes by area, would your answer have been the UK? Because it is!

New York wasn't always 'the Big Apple'. If I were to ask you what is the most famous city in the USA, your answer would probably be New York. But what if I told you that this great city was once known as 'New Orange'? This is because the Dutch captured New York from the English in 1673 and dubbed it New Orange in honour of William III of Orange. The following year the English seized control of the city once again and changed it back to its former name.

Times Square used to have a different name too. Changing the name New Orange to New York wasn't the only change this city went through. Times Square was originally called Longacre Square. Its name only changed because, in 1904, the *New York Times* moved its headquarters to the newly built Times Building nearby.

Pepsi is more powerful than you think. Pepsi was once the sixth largest military force in the world. Granted, this was only for a short period of time, but let me explain how. In 1959 American President Richard Nixon and Soviet leader Khrushchev got into a pretty heated argument about capitalism versus communism. During this discussion, the vice president of Pepsi offered Khrushchev a cup of Pepsi. This singular drink must have made an impact, because years later the Soviet Union wanted to strike a deal that would bring Pepsi products to their country permanently. The only issue was that the Soviets' money wasn't accepted throughout the world at that time. So, after many conversations about how Pepsi could have a permanent place in Russia, they went for the next 'logical' option. The Soviet Union traded a fleet of submarines and boats – specifically, 17 submarines, a cruiser, a frigate and a destroyer – for $3 billion dollars' worth of Pepsi.

Humans have slowed the rotation of Earth. Here's a frightening one for you: the Three Gorges Dam in China has actually changed the rotation of Earth. The world's largest hydroelectric power station, the Three Gorges Dam, has a total surface area of 1,045 square kilometres and holds back more than 39 trillion kilograms, or 42 billion tons, of water. Issues began with small earthquakes occurring in western China owing to the massive amount of water being held back by the dam, but it didn't stop there. Due to an effect known as the 'moment of inertia', the dam actually slows Earth's rotation, although only by 0.06 microseconds, according to calculations by NASA.

Rainbows are a full circle. What if I told you that rainbows are not the simple colourful arches we see in pictures but are instead full perfect circles? Being on the ground is not the best way to see the rest of the rainbow. You have to be lucky enough to be in the right position at the right time, and that position is, well, very high up indeed. Looking out of an aircraft window should do it.

Splashing water on your face makes your body react strangely. Something very cool happens when you splash water on your face, thanks to what is known as the 'diving reflex'. The sensory receptors within your nose slow your heart rate down and pull blood into your vital organs so you can hold your breath and swim for longer. Essentially, your body automatically prepares for a free dive. Our organs work together to protect us from the immense underwater pressure of deep water, turning us humans into efficient deep-sea diving animals.

A speck of dust is larger than you might think. To this day the following fact is incomprehensible to me: a single speck of dust is halfway between the size of an atom and the size of the entire planet earth.

There are people who look just like you. If you were determined enough, and had enough time, you would be able to travel the world and find up to seven people who look just like you – your doppelgängers. They are your biologically unrelated lookalikes.

Dogs can see in colour. It is a long-running myth that dogs can only see in black and white, but research has officially squashed this rumour. Although dogs don't see colours in the same way as the majority of humans do, they do still see colour. However, they are what we consider to be colourblind. This is because they only have two colour receptors in their eyes, whereas the majority of humans have three.

Too much sweating makes your brain shrink. Your brain is a very precious organ, which is why you need to keep it safe. Sweating for 90 minutes can temporarily shrink your brain – equivalent to one year of ageing. But drinking a glass of water will soon reverse this effect.

The human brain is faster than a Formula 1 car. Even though there's been a huge amount of research into the way the human brain works, it is surprisingly still one of the great scientific mysteries. What we do know about the brain is truly fascinating, though. Signals in the brain actually travel up to 268 miles per hour (mph), which is faster than the top speed of a Formula 1 racing car at 240 mph.

There are a lot of synapses in the brain. The complexity of the brain is almost unfathomable – there are more synapses in your brain than there are stars in the Milky Way galaxy. It's true: the number of known stars in our galaxy is approximately 200 billion, but neuroscientist researchers have found nearly one quadrillion synapses within the human brain.

The brain eats itself. What if I told you your brain is a cannibal? Your brain contains tens of billions of neurons and they require constant energy input. If you were to deprive them of energy, they would get that energy by eating themselves. One way to tell when your neurons are going crazy is if your belly rumbles with hunger. When this happens, your neurons are hungry too and they are beginning to eat parts of themselves for energy.

You are blind for 40 minutes a day. Did you know that for approximately 40 minutes a day you are blind? This is due to a process called 'saccadic masking'. When your eyes move, your brain purposely blocks your vision, which is why if you look in a mirror, you cannot see your own eyes moving. Without saccadic masking your whole life would be like watching a never-ending movie filmed on a shaky handheld camera.

You can use your body as a conductor. Have you forgotten where you parked your car? You could try finding it by using your key fob, and if that doesn't work, you could use your body to extend the signal from your key to your lost car. Place the key under your chin and open your mouth – this turns your skull into an antenna. The fluids within your head make it a good enough conductor to increase the range of your key.

Lego Minifigures outnumber humans. Currently the earth is populated by 8.06 billion human beings. However, what if I told you that there's another population of 'people' on earth whose numbers are considerably higher? They are Lego Minifigures, and there are estimated to be 10 billion of them.

There was a party for time travellers in 2009. Stephen Hawking was one of the smartest man to have ever existed, and in 2009 he conducted an experiment that could have changed humanity forever. Whereas most experiments require test tubes and chemicals, this one needed champagne, balloons and a banner. He threw a time traveller party, but he didn't send out any invitations until after it was over. He explained that he sat there for a long time but no one came. This confirmed to him that backward time travel probably isn't possible.

Mirrors can mislead you. There is a company that only sells mirrors that specifically make people look five kilograms thinner. What's more concerning is that the mirrors are responsible for 54 per cent of total sales at the retailers who use them in their stores.

There's a company that lets employees call in hungover to work. It is a widely known fact that calling in sick to work is OK, but blaming that sickness on drinking too much alcohol the night before is definitely a no-go. However, there is a company in the UK that offers 'being hungover' as a valid excuse for calling off work. In fact, the company offers four hungover days per year. So if you're lucky enough to work for Dice in Shoreditch, working hungover will be a thing of the past for you.

A bolt of lightning is hotter than the sun. A bolt of lightning can reach a staggering 29,730°C, which is five times hotter than the surface of the sun. For comparison, the sun's surface only reaches 5,730°C.

You can hear weird things in the quietest room on earth. There is a room that is so quiet it is measured in negative decibels. It is the quietest room in the world and it is in Minnesota, USA. It is so quiet you can hear your own heartbeat, and even more disturbingly, your bones moving.

There is a human toe cocktail. This drink is a *very* acquired taste. There is a bar in Yukon, the smallest and most western of Canada's three territories, that sells a 'Sourtoe Cocktail'. It consists of a shot of whiskey and a human toe floating in the glass. What's even more disturbing is that an estimated 60,000 people have tried it.

There's a country where it's legal to try to escape prison. It's widely known that if you are convicted of a crime and put in prison, until you've served your time, there's no getting out, and any attempt at escape will lead to further punishment. This is true everywhere except Mexico. Any non-violent attempts to escape a Mexican prison are not punished because 'it's human nature to want freedom'.

The most boring news day ever happened in 1930.
Many of us tune into the news every day to find out
what is happening locally or globally, but would you
ever expect to turn on your TV and be greeted by a
contentless programme? Well, this is what happened on
18 April 1930, when a BBC radio presenter announced,
'There is no news.'

Santa Claus might be real. This is probably the
most confusing fact in this entire book. In 1927 Santa
Claus was issued an actual pilot's licence by the
US government. At the same time they gave him an
assurance that runway lights would be left on bright on
Christmas Eve.

Ronald MacDonald robbed a Wendy's. There's always
rivalry going on within the fast-food industry, but one
person may have taken it to the next level. In 2005
Ronald MacDonald was arrested for robbing a Wendy's
restaurant in Manchester, New Hampshire. As funny as
it is to believe it was the actual McDonald's clown gone
rogue, there's no relation between the famed face of the
fast-food giant and the 22-year-old Ronald McDonald
who was arrested.

The most dangerous thing in Australia isn't an animal.
Think of Australia and you probably think of all the
creatures that can bite, sting or poison you, or cause
you mental trauma for the rest of your life. In fact, the
most dangerous thing on the continent isn't an animal
but a plant: *Dendrocnide macrolides*. Green and fuzzy-
leafed, this plant might seem harmless, but touching it
can leave you in agonising pain for months, if not years,
because the needles of this plant contain a potent
neurotoxin. The pain is compared to being burned by
scorching acid and it feels like electric shocks down
your spine. What makes it worse is that, during the
summer, the plant actually sheds its needles, which
means they could sting you even if you don't touch the
plant. Some have said the pain is so agonising that it
can give you suicidal thoughts, making you believe that
death itself would be a better option.

There used to be gorilla-sized lemurs. Madagascar
was once home to a genus of giant lemurs that
were very similar in size to present-day gorillas.
Archaeoindris fontoynontii inhabited Madagascar until
about 350 BC, and they were so massive that they are
thought to have been the largest primate to have ever
walked the planet.

Your phone is dirtier than a bathroom. How would you react if I told you your phone is dirtier than a public bathroom? Recent research undertaken in the USA found that there were on average more than 17,000 bacterial gene copies on the phones of the high school students who participated in the study – including pathogens such as MRSA, *Streptococcus* and even *E. coli*. That's ten times more bacteria than is found on most toilet seats.

You have probably walked past a murderer. Have you ever considered exactly who you walk past in the street every day? If not, that might change after this fact. On average in the USA, there are around 25–50 active serial killers at any one time. This is a terrifying enough concept without adding in the fact that you will walk past roughly 36 murderers in your lifetime.

Trees

Trees are immortal. There are very few things on Earth
that can be classed as immortal, but some species of
trees technically are. Now, I say 'technically' because
that isn't to say they won't die at all – they can die of
other causes, but not old age. A prime example of this
is the pine tree. In a forest in California there's a pine
tree known as Methuselah, named after the oldest
person in the Bible. This tree is nearly 5,000 years old.
In Chile there's a 3,600-year-old cypress tree, and in
Sri Lanka there's a sacred fig that was planted in the
third century BC!

Trees have a fountain of youth. How do long-lived trees
stay so youthful forever? It's very clever: the tree has the
ability to slow down the effects of ageing. It can replace
parts of itself that it loses, as well as build dead tissue
on its own. Indeed, if you were to examine a tree with
an epic lifespan, you'd find that up to 95 per cent of its
trunk might be dead, but it's still growing.

Trees can kill predators. When you think of predators, you probably think of lions or tigers, but what if I told you that trees can actually gang up on the creatures that attack them? You might not imagine that a one-on-one between a tree and a predator would go particularly well for the tree, but that's where you're wrong. Some trees can actually release an airborne chemical that signals to other trees when there are incoming threats, such as insects; it's like the trees are calling for backup. Once the signal has been received, the trees can arm themselves by producing 'tannins', a yellowish/brownish organic substance that makes their leaves taste bitter to predators. The chemical can also attract other predators or parasites to kill an invading pest. For example, when apple trees are under attack by caterpillars, the trees will release a chemical that actively attracts caterpillar-eating birds.

Trees have Wi-Fi. If you found yourself in the middle of the forest, you probably wouldn't have internet, right? Well, what if I told you that trees have their own kind of internet? Known as 'soil fungi', it is an underground system of fungi that live on the roots of many trees. Their main purpose is to help the trees absorb water and nutrients from the soil, but their wider use is to connect the entire forest. The fungi help the trees to create a huge, intricately connected platform that allows them to communicate and share resources – not dissimilar to how we use the internet. This allows much older and larger trees, known as 'mother trees', to connect to hundreds of younger trees around them, and to send them nutrients such as water and even carbon that they don't use.

Trees can make you happy. How about one last tree fact to knock your socks off? Trees have the ability to actively make us happier – no wonder you naturally feel a sense of calm when you wander through a forest. The health benefits of being in a forest are often attributed to taking a walk in the fresh air, but that isn't the whole picture. Trees like cedar, oak and pine actually give off chemical compounds known as phytoncides. Studies have shown that breathing in these phytoncides can help us fight virus-infected cells, resulting in reduced blood pressure and lower anxiety levels. It has even been suggested that breathing in phytoncides can boost our levels of anti-cancer proteins. This isn't just a myth – the Japanese have even coined the phrase 'forest bathing' to refer to a method of breathing in the chemicals that are released by forests.

Places you SHOULDN'T visit

Snake Island, Brazil

Snake Island (also known as Ilha da Queimada Grande) is located just off the coast of Brazil, but don't let its beautiful scenery, tropical weather, lush rainforests and great coastline fool you. If you're scared of snakes, like I am, this island is the ninth circle of hell.

As the name would suggest, Snake Island is home to many snakes. It is estimated that there are between 2,000 and 4,000 Golden Lancehead vipers there. If you were bitten by one of these (and being on a place called Snake Island, I wouldn't say that possibility is too far-fetched), you'd only have an hour to seek medical assistance before you found yourself shaking hands with your ancestors. The venom from a Golden Lancehead viper is three to five times more potent than that of the snakes who live on the mainland, and it contains a toxin that can melt human flesh.

Unfortunately, seeking medical attention on Snake Island isn't easy. There's no hospital or medical centre on the island; the only building is a lighthouse. And just like any lighthouse, someone once had to man it. Legend says that the last lighthouse keeper and his family, who lived there in the 1900s, did not make it off the island: snakes got into their home through open windows.

The Golden Lancehead viper grows to a maximum length of over half a metre. When you consider that there's one snake on the island for every square metre of land, you can already imagine that you wouldn't go too long without seeing one.

Golden Lancehead Vipers aren't the only snake that lives in these parts. *Dipsas albifrons*, otherwise known as Sauvage's Snail-eater, also calls Snake Island home. Thankfully, though, they are non-venomous, and as the name suggests, they feast on snails and other smaller bugs.

There is an interesting tale about how there came to be so many snakes on Snake Island. The story goes that a long time ago pirates buried their treasure on the island, and as a way to keep it safe, they put venomous snakes there too.

Perhaps unsurprisingly, given the large venomous snake population, access to the island has been outlawed. The Brazilian government strictly control any visits to Ilha da Queimada Grande, so only certain scientists are allowed to go there. But why would they want to? Well, there is a silver lining to all this horror: the venom from the Golden Lancehead viper is thought to be useful for making medicine. Studies have shown that the venom can be used for pharmaceutical purposes, as it can help with heart disease, circulation and blood clots.

23

North Sentinel Island, India

North Sentinel Island is home to the Sentinelese tribe and it tops the list of the most forbidden islands in the world. The Sentinelese tribe have inhabited the island for over 50,000 years and are now under the protection of the Indian government.

The Sentinelese tribe is one of very few tribes around the world that have managed to stay untouched by modern civilisation – and because they want to remain isolated, they are hostile towards any visitors. The tribe is thought to descend from the first human population in Africa to have migrated out of the continent.

What is truly amazing is how this tribe was barely affected by the devastating Indian Ocean earthquake of 2004 and the tsunami that followed. More than 230,000 people in countries near the Indian Ocean were killed in the disaster, and because North Sentinel Island is located in the Bay of Bengal, the Indian coastguard sent a helicopter to survey the island and check for survivors. They found that the population of the island was hardly affected, and it is thought that this is because they noticed changes in the movement of the winds and the environment around them, which helped them quickly move to higher ground to protect themselves.

However, although the population fared well, the island itself was drastically changed by the disastrous earthquake, which tilted the tectonic plate underneath the island and lifted it by up to two metres, exposing the surrounding coral reefs and drying them out. The island's terrain was extended by as much as a kilometre to the west and the south.

From afar, observations of the Sentinelese tribe have concluded that they appear to be healthy, vigorous and strong. However, the people of North Sentinel Island are highly likely to be vulnerable to modern diseases, such as the flu and measles. This is because they have not built up an immunity to these common illnesses as they have not been in contact with the rest of the world.

Living on an island in the middle of the ocean does have its drastic downsides, and making fire is one of them. It appears the Sentinelese do not have the technology or the means to create fire on their own. As a result, they rely on lightning striking the island to kindle fire. Once the fire is roaring, they guard it to prevent the embers from burning out.

In an attempt to build a rapport with the tribe, anthropologists, under the authority of the Indian government, have delivered numerous gifts to the tribespeople. They are fond of coconuts because they do not grow naturally on the island. Another gift to the tribe was a live pig, but this did not go down as well as the coconuts; the pig was speared to the ground and buried immediately. Plastic toys were met with similar caution, but metal pots and pans were accepted with open arms.

Runit Island, Marshall Islands

I would not recommend ever visiting Runit Island. Situated between Hawaii and Australia, it doesn't look like much from afar – if anything, it looks relatively peaceful. However, there is a single structure on the island: a giant concrete dome known as the 'nuclear coffin'. This dome is one of the most radiated pieces of land in the world.

Between 1948 and 1958, nuclear tests of all sorts were conducted on Runit Island by the USA. During this decade of testing, all forms of life on the island were absolutely decimated. In an attempt to help the surrounding environment, all the hazardous nuclear material was placed inside the 107-metre concrete dome, but unlike the top of the dome, the bottom was not sealed with concrete, and as a result radioactive waste is slowly leaking into the surrounding ocean. In 1979 the island was finally deemed uninhabitable.

Places you CAN'T visit

Svalbard Global Seed Vault, Norway

On the Norwegian island of Spitsbergen, deep within the Arctic Circle, sits the Global Seed Vault, otherwise known as the Doomsday Vault. This is the most important vault in all of human history, because it currently holds 100 million seeds – a complete backup of earth's food crops.

Built to survive the absolute worst-case scenario of a worldwide disaster, the contents of this vault will preserve the diversity of the world's food crops so that, if we ever needed to, we could restore the entire plant kingdom. The vault can withstand earthquakes and explosions and was strategically placed on the side of a mountain so that even if all the ice on earth melts, the vault will remain uncompromised above sea level. The many seed samples are stored at a cosy –18°C to ensure their longevity.

The first withdrawal from the 'seed bank of the world' was made by Syria. This enabled them to recreate an international research centre in Aleppo that had been lost during a war and was previously used to store genetic material from crops. Today this is of vital importance in war-torn and drought-affected Syria.

Catacombs of Paris, France

There is a two-mile section of the Paris catacombs that is open to the public, but the remainder of the 200-mile-long underground system of complex pathways and tunnels is illegal for the public to access. The open sections are maintained, surveyed and easy to navigate.

But I know you don't want to read about the legal section, so how about I tell you about the forbidden 200 miles of terrifying tunnels? There are several secret entrances to the tunnels scattered across Paris, and locals are known to enter frequently to explore the tunnels. These trespassing explorers have even managed to map out and memorise hundreds of entry points.

The catacombs of Paris have a skin-crawling nickname: the 'Empire of Death'. This is because they are one large underground burial system. But it's not all doom and gloom under the streets of the city of love. Some 'cataphiles' report a warm, friendly atmosphere down there, with people playing music and enjoying a drink. The communities formed in these tunnels have been known to throw parties for birthdays and Halloween (that one actually makes sense), carnivals, concerts and even dinners.

Room 39, North Korea

Room 39 in North Korea is one of the most secret places in what is arguably the most secretive state in the world. It is located within the Workers' Party building in Pyongyang. Not much is known about what goes on within that room, but the secrecy surrounding it suggests it could have something to do with raising funds through commercial enterprises – both legal and illegal – ranging from counterfeiting money to selling gold, drugs and weapons. It is also speculated that Room 39 could be behind the counterfeiting of high-quality $100 'supernote' bills.

The Coca-Cola vault, Atlanta, USA

It may be hard to believe that one of the best-kept secrets in the world is the Coca-Cola recipe, but it has remained a trade secret for 130 years because it is stored in a large security vault.

The recipe has changed locations several times over the years. In 1920 it ended up under strict lock and key at a New York bank, then in 1925 it was transferred to the Trust Company Bank in Atlanta. Finally, in 2011, the company made the decision to move the famous recipe to an Atlanta museum. To this day it has never been revealed how many people know the true formula for Coca-Cola.

CHAPTER 2:

SPACE

Space, like the ocean, is a place that terrifies even the bravest of humans, and as we have taken our metaphorical first steps into the deep unknown, we have discovered distances we cannot comprehend, planets that seem impossible and wandering objects that could decimate all life. Here are the craziest space facts you never knew.

General facts

There are millions of black holes in our galaxy.
Astronomers estimate that there are around 100 million
black holes wandering the Milky Way. In an unlikely but
not completely implausible scenario, if a wandering
black hole were to pass through our solar system, Earth
could be flung out into deep space. The closest black
hole astronomers have discovered goes by the name of
Gaia BH1, and it is approximately 1,560 light years away
from wherever you are currently reading this.

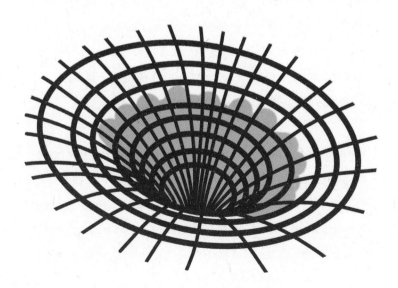

There are 60 known rogue planets in the Milky Way.
We tend to think of planets as being attached ever so
comfortably to a star, within a solar system like ours,
but that isn't always the case. Rogue planets are free-
floating; they drift through space without a parent star.
They are large planetary objects that have been ejected
from their solar systems and are no longer bound to any
star or substellar object. A rogue planet has no orbit,
meaning it can move wherever or collide with whatever
it wants. What may be even more terrifying is that rogue
planets travel at hypervelocity, moving through space at
up to 30 million miles per hour, or roughly 13,000km/s.

You have never been in the same place twice. Since
you were born, you have never been in the same place
twice. Think about it: the Milky Way galaxy is travelling
through space at around 550km/s. That means that every
year our galaxy, and therefore Earth, moves 17 billion
kilometres away from where it was one year ago.

The forecast is sideways-raining glass. I know we have
experienced some out-of-the-ordinary weather here on
earth, but have you ever imagined a place where glass
rains sideways? Well, on the exoplanet we've snappily
called HD 189733b, that absolute nightmare fuel exists.

Earth was once hit by another planet. A roughly Mars-sized planet by the name of Theia crashed into the early-forming Earth approximately 4.5 billion years ago, and the resulting ejected debris formed the Moon. The collision is believed to have brought water to Earth, as Theia was an ice-encrusted planet, and so large quantities of water were transferred from Theia onto the early Earth by this violent collision. The reason Theia contained large deposits of water was because it formed in the more frigid outer solar system, rather than the inner solar system where it is much hotter and drier.

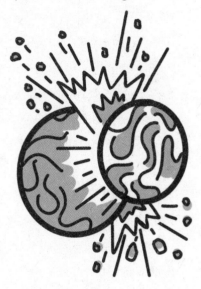

Planet J1407b is Saturn × 640. Of all the planets in our solar system, Saturn is probably the most easily recognisable. Its wide, flat rings extend out over 75,000 miles from the planet itself and they are a staple of our solar system. Well, let me introduce you to 'Saturn on steroids' – an exoplanet 434 light years from Earth that has a massive system of circumplanetary rings about 640 times the size of Saturn's.

There's a planet where it rains rubies and sapphires.
Hat-P-7b, otherwise known as Kepler-2b, is a celestial
body where it rains rubies and sapphires. This is because
the clouds on this planet are infused with a crystalline
form of aluminium oxide – the same mineral that produces
the precious gems we find on earth. If you spent just one
afternoon on this planet, you would be rich beyond your
wildest dreams. However, it would also be warmer than
the most intense sauna you've ever been inside, as Hat-
P-7b reaches temperatures of approximately 2,600°C, so
essentially you would just evaporate.

Venus has secrets. Although planets such as Hat-P-7b
and HD 189773b are a considerable distance away
from Earth, there is one closer to home that also has
weather we couldn't imagine. On our neighbour Venus
it actually snows metal. There is a layer of snow beneath
the thick clouds of Venus, on top of its mountains.
However, because temperatures can reach 462°C, snow
as we know it physically cannot exist there. Instead the
mountains are capped with two types of metal: galena
and bismuthinite.

Metal sticks together in space. If two pieces of the
same type of metal touch in space, they will immediately
be permanently stuck together. This phenomenon is

known as 'cold welding'. Unlike on Earth, where heat is required to fuse metals, this process takes place in space because of the lack of oxygen surrounding the metals; in the vacuum of space, their atoms essentially can't tell that they're part of two separate pieces, and so they become conjoined.

There are more moves in a game of chess than atoms in the universe. The observable universe is so vast that it is difficult to truly comprehend how many atoms make it up. But what if I told you that there are more potential moves you could make in a game of chess than there are atoms in the universe? For some context, the estimated number of atoms in the observable universe is between 10^{78} and 10^{82}, whereas the number of possible moves in a game of chess is so massive that it is known as the 'Shannon number', equalling 10^{120}.

Russia is larger than Pluto. We often look at our planet within the vast emptiness of space and feel terrified by how small we truly are, but Pluto – the planet famously demoted from planetary status – has a smaller total surface area than the entire country of Russia. The surface of Pluto is 16.7 million square kilometres, whereas Russia's surface area is about 17 million square kilometres.

You could fold a piece of paper to reach the Moon.

You may know that each time you fold a piece of paper
its thickness doubles – this is exponential growth. But
did you know that if you folded a piece of paper 42
times, it could reach from Earth to the surface of the
Moon? That's difficult to comprehend, but even more
unimaginable is what would happen if you folded a
piece of paper 103 times. The thickness of that piece
of paper would be equivalent to the diameter of the
observable universe – which, for context, is 93 billion
light years. If you want the maths, here it is: the average
thickness of a piece of paper is one-tenth of a millimetre,
or 0.1mm. By folding a piece of paper once it becomes
0.2mm, and folding a third time the thickness is now
0.4mm. This is what is known as exponential growth,
and it is thanks to exponential growth that if you were to
keep on folding a piece of paper perfectly in half, things
would get interesting very quickly.

The Moon used to be alive. The Moon wasn't always the floating, lifeless cosmic rock we know it to be today. At one point in time you might have considered it to be alive thanks to its volcanoes. It is believed that volcanoes may have been erupting on the Moon during the Cretaceous Period, the heyday of the dinosaurs. We know this because we have estimated the age of the Moon's landscape by looking at its craters. There would have been so many eruptions at that time that there would have been an ocean of magma on the Moon's surface for close to 200 million years.

A mountain top is the closest place on Earth to the Moon. If you want to get as close to the Moon as possible without making friends at NASA or SpaceX, you will have to climb Mount Chimborazo in Ecuador, the closest place on Earth to the Moon. This is because there is a bulge on Earth where the mountain is located, which makes it the closest point to outer space. Now, generally speaking, the Moon and Earth are 250,000 miles apart, and although being at the very top of Ecuador Mount would bring you approximately 13 miles closer to the Moon, you would still have a bit of a way to go.

Mount Everest is small compared to Mars's biggest mountain. It's hard to imagine a natural structure that can compare to Mount Everest. Well, let me present to you Mars's Olympus Mons, the largest volcano in our solar system. Reaching a staggering three times the height of Everest and as wide as the country of France, it towers 16 miles above the surrounding plains of the red planet. As a comparison, Hawaii's Mauna Loa, the tallest volcano on Earth, only rises 6.3 miles above the sea floor.

We wouldn't know right away if the Sun exploded. The Sun is 93 million miles away from Earth, which is a vast distance, but have we truly considered it? Let's say the Sun was to explode when you reached the end of this sentence. Boom. You'd look up at the sky and the Sun would still look perfectly normal, right? Correct! You wouldn't know for sure that the Sun had exploded for another 8 minutes and 20 seconds. Even after the explosion, the light show could still only travel at the speed of light, and it takes light 8 minutes and 20 seconds to travel the immense distance between the Sun and Earth.

The size of our solar system is mind-boggling. The scale of space is hard to comprehend, but I'm going to try and give you some perspective on the scale of our small pocket of space. If you were to fly to the Moon, it would take you approximately three days, and if you were to fly to Mars, it would take you approximately seven months. However, if you were to fly to the outermost planetary object within our solar system, Pluto, it would take you 9.5 years – already we have gone from three days to nearly an entire decade.

But Pluto is not where the solar system ends. If you wanted to get to the very edge of the solar system, you would have to pass through the Oort Cloud, which is essentially a cloud of comets in interstellar space. The sheer size of the Oort Cloud is unimaginable: to reach the inner edge of it would take you 300 years, but to fly beyond it would take nearly 30,000 years. And that's just our solar system.

Space has a smell. Have you ever stopped to think about what space smells like? Well, strangely enough, there is actually an answer to this. While there isn't any sound in space, there is a particular smell. Many astronauts who have ventured into the deep unknown have described the odour of space in different ways. Some say it smells like hot metal, while others describe it as being like welding fumes, gunpowder or even seared steak. I can't say I would be too disappointed with that last one.

There are more stars in the universe than grains of sand on earth. This famous idea came from the astronomer Carl Sagan. Let's work it out using the very latest geological studies, shall we? Scientists have calculated that earth holds 7.5 sextillion (7,500,000,000,000,000,000) grains of sand – that's a lot of sand! And using astronomical calculations made by studying nearby galaxies, it has been estimated that our universe contains at least 70 septillion (700,000,000, 000,000,000,000,000) stars.

The Moon is leaving us. Our closest celestial body, the Moon, used to look significantly bigger from here on Earth. When the Moon formed it was actually around ten times closer to Earth than it is today. Just imagine that for a second – looking up at the Moon and it looking ten times larger than it does now. Recent computer simulations have suggested that the Moon could have even been 12–19 times closer, or at a distance of 20,000–30,000km compared to the 384,000km it is today. The reason it is further from Earth today is not because of a cosmic argument – in fact, the Moon is constantly spinning away from us. It gets 3.78cm further away from Earth each year (roughly the same rate at which your fingernails grow).

The strangest items to have gone to space

Over the course of human history, only around 550 humans have ever ventured into space. However, a number of questionable items have made their way to the final frontier. Let me explain ...

A lightsaber. *Star Wars* captured the hearts of the world with its tales of space exploration, and in 2007 the actual prop lightsaber that was used by Mark Hamill when he played Luke Skywalker in *Episode VI: Return of the Jedi* was taken into space by astronauts.

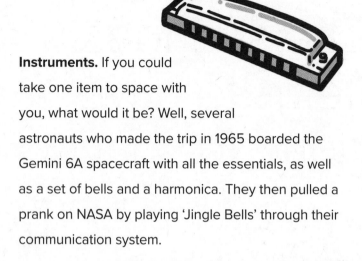

Instruments. If you could take one item to space with you, what would it be? Well, several astronauts who made the trip in 1965 boarded the Gemini 6A spacecraft with all the essentials, as well as a set of bells and a harmonica. They then pulled a prank on NASA by playing 'Jingle Bells' through their communication system.

Unique foods. A plethora of foods have been taken into the unknown, including beef jerky and preserved foods. However, the world's first space delivery was actually conducted by Pizza Hut in 2001. To ensure it would not spoil on its long adventure, the pizza was heavily salted, and it was delivered to the Russians on the International Space Station at a cost of approximately $1 million.

The world's most popular toy. NASA and Lego collaborated to create Lego figures of the Roman god Jupiter, Jupiter's wife, Juno, and Galileo Galilei, which were taken on board the Juno spacecraft. This was done to create a news story that would interest students in schools.

Voyager 1 and 2 Golden Records. These might be the most fascinating objects ever sent into space, and they're something humans will most likely never get back. During the 1970s Carl Sagan, a famous astronomer, asked an important question: if a spacecraft humans sent into space was ever picked up by an extraterrestrial intelligence, how would they know it came from Earth? This question led to the creation of the Voyager Golden Records. When NASA's Voyager 1 and 2 space probes were launched in 1977, Sagan and his team created and fitted a 12-inch golden record to each craft, complete with instructions on how to play it. The records include 115 images in analogue form, greetings spoken in 55 languages, the 'sound of Earth' and a 90-minute selection of music throughout the ages from around the world.

A message to extraterrestrials. Pioneer 10 and 11 both carried small metal plaques with information on them, including their time and place of origin. The plaques provide the location of humanity within our galaxy, as well as depicting a naked man and woman. Well, now that they know our location and anatomy, let's hope every movie in the history of cinema has been wrong about aliens.

The most terrifying objects in space

The biggest comet is the size of a planet. Let's talk about mega-comets. In 2021 the biggest ever comet made its appearance in our little neighbourhood, the solar system. Decimating the previous record by 50 times, this comet was a terrifying 85 miles across and was known as Comet C, or 2014UN271. This comet was so big that when it was first discovered it was classified as a minor planet. But you can rest easy – the closest it is predicted to get to us anytime soon is in 2031 when it will come to within 1.6 billion kilometres from Earth.

We can track asteroids for future impacts. There are asteroids out in our solar system, and it is important that we find and track as many as we possibly can to try to avoid the fate the dinosaurs suffered 66 million years ago. This can be achieved through asteroid redirection, which was successfully trialled for the first time on 26 September 2022, when NASA's DART spacecraft altered an asteroid's orbit. The mission targeted the asteroid Dimorphos, causing an impact that reduced the time it takes for Dimorphos to orbit its larger asteroid companion by 32 minutes. This mission showed that asteroid redirection is possible. The search for asteroids has gone well, and scientists believe that 90 per cent of planet-killers and around 50 per cent of city-killers have been found. However, the European Space Agency's Gaia space telescope revealed in 2022 that there are approximately ten times more asteroids within the solar system than astronomers previously thought. New data sets show a staggering 154,741 extra objects, most of them being asteroids.

The Andromeda galaxy will collide with the Milky Way. The Andromeda galaxy will give you a complete nightmare makeover. Only 2.5 million light years away from Earth, Andromeda might seem like any other normal spiral galaxy. However, the Milky Way and

Andromeda share something: a trajectory path. In 3–5 billion years Andromeda, the largest galaxy in our Local Group, will collide with our Milky Way. This will result in an even larger galaxy being formed, but not a spiral galaxy like we and Andromeda are today – rather it will form a giant elliptical galaxy.

The largest black hole. Everyone's most feared unknown in space is the black hole: the crushed remnants of a massive star that exploded as a supernova. They range in size from moderately scary to downright stomach-turning, life-questioning, therapy-needing nightmare fuel. However, the object known as TON 618 has features that are so exaggerated scientists find it hard to comprehend such an object exists. This is an ultra-massive black hole with a mass equivalent to that of 66,000 million Suns. The radius of this black hole is approximately 207 billion kilometres – that is the length of 11 solar systems lined up side by side. Even more horrifying, Earth could technically fit within it 26,000,000,000,000,000,000,000 times.

The end of
the universe

It's easy to convince ourselves that the universe and its infinite wonder will be around forever, but that is not the case. Just like everything else, the universe will have an ending. But just how will quite literally everything suddenly cease to exist? Scientists have come up with multiple possibilities for how the universe will meet its fate, so let's go through them.

The big crunch. This possibility is based on Einstein's theory of general relativity. As we know, the universe is constantly expanding, but this will not continue forever. Think about the universe like an elastic band: when we stretch the band out there comes a point, at its biggest, when it will no longer expand and we must let it go. This is the concept behind the big crunch: one day the universe will stop expanding and collapse into itself, pulling everything that exists in the universe in with it, and eventually forming the biggest ever black hole.

The big rip. This idea came from scientists in the late 1990s who began to look even deeper into space than ever before. They realised that distant objects are moving away from us at an ever-accelerating rate. Scientists predict that if the universe continues to accelerate at this rate, it will reach a point where the forces that hold it together will be overcome by dark energy and will quite literally rip apart. Galaxies will be pulled apart, followed by star systems; planets will be torn from their stars, and the stars themselves will be ripped apart. And it won't stop there. All atomic and molecular forces will meet their demise too – electrons splitting from atoms all the way down to quarks, and anything that is even smaller will be completely shredded out of existence.

The big bounce. This is a slightly more optimistic look at the end of the universe, but still very much a hypothetical scientific model. This model explains that, although the universe will end, it also won't end. I know that doesn't really make sense at first glance, but let me explain. Similar to the big crunch, there will come a point when the universe can no longer continue its ever-expanding adventure and will collapse back in on itself. However, rather than permanently deleting everything from existence for good, this will instead cause another big bang, creating a cyclical, endless universe.

The big freeze. This one doesn't sound pleasant as it is also known as 'heat death'. No, the universe won't suddenly burst into flames, destroying everything in it once and for all. Rather, the British physicist Lord Kelvin, who originally proposed the idea in the 1850s, referred to this theory as the loss of mechanical energy. Essentially, the more the universe expands, the cooler it gets. This comes from the second law of thermodynamics. The theory is that, one day, the universe will become so vast and energy will be spread so thin that the universe will just freeze. No new stars will form, and time and space will become an endless void in which nothing ever happens.

CHAPTER 3:

OCEAN

The ocean, like space, is truly a domain of mysteries and oddities. Even though it sits on the same planet as us, we have only explored a mere 5 per cent of it. But although most of its secrets are yet to be discovered by humans, there's enough nightmare fuel in that 5 per cent to scare the bejesus out of you, as this chapter proves.

General facts

Point Nemo is the loneliest point on Earth. There is a point in the Pacific Ocean called Point Nemo. *Nemo* in Latin means 'no one' or 'nobody', and that translation could not be more accurate – this is the point in the ocean that is furthest from land.

Fish can fly. Flying fish can launch themselves out of the water at 35mph and glide for 200m, the length of two football fields.

The ocean is an infectious place. Just one millilitre of ocean water can contain approximately 10 million viruses.

Sharks are older than trees. Sharks have been around for hundreds of millions of years, appearing in the fossil record even before trees existed. The first evidence of seeded plants appeared in the fossil record approximately 360 million years ago, whereas the earliest known evidence of sharks dates back to more than 420 million years ago.

The ocean is the world's largest graveyard. The ocean is the most popular place to dispose of bodies, so much so that it holds more human remains than all the graveyards on earth combined.

The ocean could make you rich. While the last fact may have had you firmly planting your feet on dry land, this next one will have you reaching for your snorkelling gear. According to the National Ocean Service, our oceans contain 20 million tons of gold. The only issue is that the gold in the ocean is so diluted that its concentration is very small. However, if we found a way to collect it all, there would be enough for every person on the planet to be given four kilograms of gold. As the National Ocean Service explains, on average each litre of seawater contains about 13 billionths of a gram of gold.

There are rivers at the bottom of the ocean.

The ocean fascinates and terrifies many of us, and that is all too true thanks to this next fact: at the bottom of the ocean there are flowing rivers and lakes. Let me explain how that is even possible. Essentially, when saltwater combines with hydrogen sulfide, the mixture becomes denser than the water around it. As a result, it sinks to the bottom and forms a lake or river. But let me warn you, these 'brine pools' do not have any oxygen, so as well as being very salty, they are toxic.

You swim in fish remains. I feel like I should put a warning here, because after reading this you are actively going to want to stay on land the next time you go to the beach. When you swim, or even take a photo of something underwater, you are almost guaranteed to see small white specks floating around. We don't tend to take much notice of this; it's just disturbed sand resettling, right? Wrong! This is what is known as 'marine snow', a shower of organic material falling from the upper waters to the depths below. When a plant or animal dies and begins to decay, it will fall towards the sea floor. Not only are these specks parts of literal dead animals, they're also faecal matter, sand, soot and other inorganic dust. I would recommend keeping your mouth closed during your next swim.

The deepest point on earth is in the ocean. The
Mariana Trench is the deepest point in the ocean, at
approximately 11,000 metres. To give you a sense
of how deep that is, if you look up the next time a
commercial plane flies over you, the distance between
you and that plane is approximately the same as the
distance from you to the very bottom of the ocean,
if you were standing on a boat over the Mariana Trench.

Humans have littered the bottom of the ocean.
Surprisingly, the depth to the bottom of the ocean isn't
the craziest fact I can share about the Mariana Trench.
During a dive that reached nearly 11,000 metres,
thanks to a submersible that protected its passengers
from the immense pressure outside, a plastic shopping
bag was found.

**You couldn't swim to the bottom of the Mariana
Trench.** Don't even consider being a good person and
trying to retrieve that plastic bag. The deeper you go
into the watery abyss, the greater the pressure; there
is no way you would physically make it down there. But
for argument's sake, let's assume you could stand at the
very bottom of the Mariana Trench – it would feel like
holding up nearly 50 jumbo jets.

The ocean is the world's biggest museum. There are more historical artefacts underwater than in all of the world's museums combined.

The ocean is home to millions of shipwrecks. Wondering where all the artefacts in the ocean come from? Many come from ships that have been lost at sea. There are estimated to be approximately 3 million shipwrecks at the bottom of the ocean.

The earth exists in complete darkness. This statement isn't as far-fetched and ludicrous as you might immediately believe. Oceans have an average depth of over 3,600 metres, and light waves can only penetrate up to 100 metres of water. This means that everything below this point exists in complete darkness. Seeing as water makes up most of the planet, most of the earth exists in absolute darkness all the time.

The ocean can make us ill. The ocean makes up approximately 71 per cent of the earth's surface, and it is strange to think that it can make humans very ill. In fact, it is littered with bacteria, and scientists aren't sure how many illnesses can be picked up from it. To get you started though, they have confirmed that you can catch hepatitis, Legionnaires' disease, MRSA, gastroenteritis and pink eye. This is because humans treat the ocean like a dumping ground.

The ocean can also make us better. Seawater is overflowing with minerals such as potassium, magnesium chloride and sodium. These can make our hair and skin look and feel better. They can also help us fight infection, reduce inflammation and heal small cuts and grazes. On top of that, because sea air has a high salt content, it is quite thick, so when we breathe it in, it can help clear our throat and respiratory system. Due to the properties of the sea air, it is also known to keep us awake and more energetic during the day.

The world's largest living structure is in the ocean. The ocean is home to many forms of life, including the world's largest living structure: the Great Barrier Reef off the coast of Australia. Extending a massive 1,429 miles, this huge structure is visible from outer space. It is composed of billions of tiny organisms known as coral polyps and it is home to a unique range of ecological communities, habitats and species, all of which make the reef one of the most complex natural ecosystems in the world.

Icebergs are bigger than you think. A large iceberg from Antarctica contains more than 76 billion litres of water. This amount of water could conceivably supply 1 million people with drinking water for up to five years. This possibility has actually intrigued a company in the United Arab Emirates, and they plan to begin towing icebergs from Antarctica to the coast for this reason. This is because the country only receives an average of ten centimetres of rainfall each year and is at risk of serious drought within the next 25 years.

Tsunamis are horrifying. While the ocean is a beautiful place full of fascinating creatures, it can also be a place of great horror. Triggered by seismic events, tsunamis – also known as seismic sea waves or tidal waves – can move across the ocean at speeds up to 500mph where the ocean depth reaches 3.7 miles. To put that into perspective, the average speed of a commercial plane is between 550 and 580mph.

The USA is underwater. The USA has an area of 9,526,468 square kilometres, but what if I told you that 50 per cent of the country is underwater? This is because its borders do not stop where the land ends. In fact, they expand 200 nautical miles out from the shore.

Melted ice could drown the Statue of Liberty. Climate change is causing the melting of the icecaps, but do you know by how much sea levels would rise if all the ice on earth melted? NASA's Jet Propulsion Laboratory estimates the sea would rise 80 metres, which is equivalent to the height of a 26-storey building, or just a bit shorter than the Statue of Liberty.

There'll soon be more plastic than fish in the ocean.
It is estimated that by 2050 the amount of plastic in the
ocean will outweigh the fish. Humans currently drop
around 8 million metric tons of plastic into the ocean
every single year, and if this continues at that rate, by
2050 there will be more plastic in the ocean than fish.

Atlantic Ocean

You can cross the Atlantic in a balloon. People have tried crazy things to cross the Atlantic over the years, but this might take the metaphorical cake. Many people have attempted to make the crossing in balloons, but to this day only one has been successful. In 1978 Ben Abruzzo and Maxie Anderson attempted to cross the Atlantic in a hot air balloon called the Double Eagle II. Departing from Presque Isle, Maine, the balloon landed 137 hours later in a barley field near Paris. The 11-storey-tall, helium-filled balloon kept the pilots alive as they survived off hot dogs and canned sardines.

The tides can get as high as a building. We don't usually consider the height of the tides; typically when we're at the beach they aren't anything to marvel at. However, this is very different in bays around the Atlantic Ocean, where they can reach 15–18m, approximately equal to the height of a six-storey building.

There are Jacuzzis in the ocean. It's not just deep-sea creatures or overwhelming pressure that could make you meet your end in the depths of the ocean; the planet itself can do this too. Hydrothermal vents are found on the ocean floor and they are known to emit hot, dark plumes of water, which are incredibly high in sulfur content and have been known to form chimney-like structures up to 18 storeys tall. They are not relaxing like the Jacuzzi in your favourite spa, though, as they can heat up the water to 400°C.

The monster from *Finding Nemo* exists in real life. We all remember that scene in *Finding Nemo* where Dory and Marlin tell themselves to 'just keep swimming' into the darkness of the ocean and suddenly encounter a horrendous monster of a fish with a 'light bulb' attached to its head. This is not something from Pixar's imagination – it is real and it's known as an anglerfish. Commonly referred to as 'sea devils', you soon get the picture that these fish are not friends in real life.

The world's largest waterfall is underwater. When we think of waterfalls, we think of Niagara Falls, but have you ever thought about a waterfall under the ocean? Well, beneath the waters of the Denmark Strait lies the world's biggest waterfall. You might be wondering how a waterfall could exist underwater. It forms when colder, denser water from the Nordic Seas comes into contact with warmer, lighter water from the Irminger Sea. The cold water descends to the ocean floor in a downward flow of around 5 million cubic metres per second. Niagara Falls' flow rate is only approximately 2,407 cubic metres per second. The Denmark Strait is 3,500 metres tall, which is more than three times the height of Angel Falls, the tallest land-based waterfall.

The Mediterranean was once empty. As we know, the Mediterranean Sea is connected by the Strait of Gibraltar to the Atlantic Ocean. However, this was not the case some 5 million years ago. The Mediterranean used to be a completely dry basin. When you consider that, on average, the sea as we know it now is 4,000–5,000 metres deep, it's hard to imagine that it was once a very deep, dry valley that separated the continents of Europe, Africa and Asia, until a cataclysmic flood, known as the Zanclean flood, began and water from the Atlantic poured through the Strait of Gibraltar and filled the basin. It is estimated that the basin filled up in only two years thanks to the massive torrent of water.

It's about to get colder. If you live anywhere in Europe, you probably won't like this next fact. Climate change is impacting the Atlantic Ocean and it could put Northern Europe into a deep freeze (even though we already know it's way too cold over here). Climate change affects the thermohaline circulation of the Atlantic Ocean. Essentially, this system balances ocean temperatures by keeping warm and cool currents moving in the right directions. However, this process is slowing down. If the current were to stop bringing enough warm water to Europe, a section of the continent could see a massive drop in temperature.

Pacific Ocean

Sharks can live inside volcanoes. Sharks are some of the most recognisable predators ever to have roamed this planet. However, you may not know that they can adapt to many environments. For example, would you expect any creature to live and thrive inside a volcano, let alone a species of shark? As it turns out, in 2015 a scientific expedition to Kavachi found that two species of shark, including hammerheads, were living within a submerged crater. The water conditions there are not normal: within the crater are supermarine plumes of superheated acidic water, which usually contain volcanic rock fragments, particulate matter and sulfur. Since this revelation, the crater has been nicknamed 'Sharkcano'.

The Pacific Ocean is larger than the moon. The Pacific Ocean is huge. To give you some perspective, at the very widest point, from Indonesia all the way to Colombia, the Pacific Ocean is wider than the moon – and not even just slightly, but by quite a lot. The total expanse of the water is 12,300 miles across, which is a staggering five times the diameter of the moon.

There is a shark cafe. What if I told you that sharks have their own underwater cafe? In 2002 scientists discovered an area in a remote section of the Pacific Ocean where coastal great white sharks migrate in the winter. This area is located partway between Baja California and Hawaii. This area was nicknamed 'White Shark Cafe' because they migrate there for food – primarily squid – and to mate.

There is a garbage patch in the Pacific. The Pacific Ocean has been very negatively impacted by humanity, and this can be clearly seen in the Great Pacific Garbage Patch. This patch consists of an ever-growing collection of human refuse, as well as marine debris, including water bottles, tyres, desk chairs and mobile phones. The Great Pacific Garbage Patch contains around 2 trillion pieces of plastic and accounts for one-third of all the plastic pollution in the world's oceans. There are five known garbage patches in the oceans: one in the Indian Ocean and two each in the Atlantic and Pacific Oceans. The Pacific Garbage Patch, however, is the largest of them all.

The ocean is shrinking. You should probably know that every single year the Pacific Ocean is shrinking by approximately 2.5 centimetres. This is due to the effects of plate tectonics. But while the Pacific Ocean is shrinking, the Atlantic Ocean is growing by roughly the same amount every year.

Somebody discovered the Pacific Ocean. Now of course, there is no way to know who the first person to lay eyes upon an entire ocean was but we do know that Vasco Nunez de Balboa was the first European to discover and sail in the Pacific Ocean. He was leading an expedition in search of gold in 1513 when he spotted the ocean. Vasco claimed it and all its lands for Spain.

The Pacific Ocean contains a ring of fire. A terrifying fact about the Pacific Ocean is that it contains 75 per cent of the world's volcanoes. Located around the ocean's basin, together they are known as the 'Ring of Fire'. As well as volcanoes, this area is also prone to earthquakes and other disturbances. Ferdinand Magellan described the ocean as a 'peaceful sea', but thanks to the existence of the Pacific Ring of Fire and one of the most famous eruptions – the 1883 Krakatoa eruption, which killed almost 37,000 people – I hardly agree.

There are endangered species in the Pacific Ocean.

The Pacific Ocean is terrifying, and having read this far you might want to stay as far away from it as you can, but we also need to protect it as it is home to at least six known endangered species, which include whales, sea turtles, sea otters, seals and sea lions. Many species live in the Pacific, but activists and scientists are becoming concerned about the future of marine life. These species depend and thrive on the balance of the ocean ecosystem, but due to multiple factors – such as hunters, an increase in natural predators and a decrease in natural prey, and increasing oil pollution – their populations are being severely affected.

The first human crossing happened in 3000 BC.

The Pacific Ocean has been of massive significance to humanity for a very long time. Although it was only discovered by Europeans in the 1500s, some have explored it for much longer. In fact, humans have used the Pacific Ocean for migration since around 3000 BC. It was during this time that humans began to embark on voyages across parts of the Pacific, specifically around Taiwan, where people crossed the ocean for trade and migration with the use of canoes.

Arctic Ocean

The Arctic Ocean is the shallowest ocean. Of all the oceans in the world, the Arctic Ocean is the shallowest, reaching an average depth of 1,038 metres.

The Arctic Ocean contains a country-sized iceberg. The largest Arctic iceberg is known as Iceberg B-15 and it measures approximately 183 miles long and 23 miles wide. It is larger than the whole island of Jamaica.

The famous Titanic iceberg may have originated here. The *Titanic* sank due to a collision with an iceberg, and this iceberg may have broken away from a glacier in the Arctic Ocean.

Indian Ocean

The Indian Ocean is millions of years old. It is believed that the Indian Ocean formed into its current configuration approximately 36 million years ago.

The Indian Ocean contains a lost continent. I bet you didn't know about this: explorers have found a piece of a continent that is now covered with lava located under the island of Mauritius. Further research suggests that this lost piece of crust is from the supercontinent of Gondwanaland, which existed on earth 200 million years ago. They have since decided to name the lost landmass Mauritia.

There is also a garbage patch in the Indian Ocean. The Indian Ocean is unfortunately very heavily polluted. In fact, there are over 1 trillion pieces of rubbish floating there, in what is known as the Indian Ocean garbage patch. It spans over 5 million square kilometres and spreads from Australia to the Mozambique Channel. The patch mainly consists of plastic rubbish.

The Indian Ocean is very dangerous. Although fascinating and full of resources, the Indian Ocean is also prone to natural disasters, such as cyclones, floods, earthquakes and tsunamis. There are multiple factors that cause all these natural disasters to occur within the Indian Ocean: evaporated vapour turning into rain, and the movement of tectonic plates. In fact, since 1970 there has been a 470 per cent increase in natural calamities there.

Human activities could destroy the Indian Ocean completely. This area of the world is used as a trade route as it connects many major landmasses. However, continuous oil extraction and transportation results in many oil spills that pollute the Indian Ocean every year. The most heavily polluted areas of the ocean are the Red Sea, the Persian Gulf and the Arabian Sea.

CHAPTER 4:

GEOGRAPHY

I can pretty much guarantee that no geography lesson in school taught you any of these facts. I wish you luck as you dive into the craziest, wildest facts about the world we live in that you had no idea were true.

UK

Brits drink a lot of tea.
When you think of British
people, what's the first
thing that comes to mind?
A lovely warm cup of tea.
It may be a stereotype
that we only drink tea in

the UK, but there's some truth to it. In fact, this must be
the nation's favourite refreshment because every year
British people consume 36 billion cups of tea.

The oldest subway station is in London. There are
over 180 subway systems in 56 countries across the
world, but did you know that London's 'Tube' is the
oldest? The London Underground officially opened its
doors on 10 January 1863.

Millions of people use the Tube. The London
Underground has a total of 11 lines that are used by
5 million passengers every day.

Mosquitos have invaded the London Underground.
Those 5 million passengers ought to be careful, because there is a subspecies of mosquito that is unique to the London Underground and it goes by the name *Culex pipiens molestus*. That's right, the pesky critters we have to worry about while on a summer holiday have decided to keep eating away at us even when we're deep underground.

The world's shortest flight takes less than a minute.
Did you know that the UK is home to the world's shortest flight? In Scotland you can grab a flight with an average air time of just 2 minutes and 40 seconds, from the tiny island of Westray to the even smaller island of Papa Westray. If the winds are just right that day, the time from take-off to touchdown can even be as short as 53 seconds.

Animals need passports. Believe it or not, it isn't just humans who need a passport to travel out of the UK — horses, donkeys, mules and zebras all require them too. The document includes information such as the name of the owner and the animal's vaccination records, as well as species, breed and colour.

Cab drivers are geographical geniuses. London cab drivers are borderline geographical geniuses. If you aspire to be a cab driver in London, you will undergo a test that is so intense it will physically alter your brain. The test includes: memorising every road, turning and intersection on 320 sample runs; memorising all 25,000 streets, roads, lanes and yards within a six-mile radius of Charing Cross; and memorising over 20,000 individual landmarks and points of interest that tourists or locals might want to go to, such as museums, theatres, clubs, pubs and cemeteries.

The UK used to speak French. Do you speak French, or have you ever wanted to? Well, if you were living in Britain during the years 1066–1362, you would have done, as French was the official language of England for nearly 300 years following the Norman Conquest led by William the Conqueror. English was only made the official language of the courts in 1362.

Big Ben is not a clock. This is going to be a revolutionary fact for some of you. If I asked you what Big Ben is, you'd probably say 'that massive clock tower in London', but you would be wrong. The tower that everyone posts photographs of on Instagram with #BigBen is technically incorrect, as until 2012 it was known as St Stephen's Tower. After 2012 it was renamed Elizabeth Tower in honour of the Queen's Diamond Jubilee. Big Ben is the name of the bell that chimes within the tower, not the tower itself.

The UK had the shortest war in history. The UK has been involved in many wars over the years, but have you ever wondered what the shortest war in history was and who it involved? Thankfully I have the answer for you right here. The war was named the Anglo-Zanzibar War of 1896 and it is recognised by Guinness World Records as the shortest war in history because it only lasted 38 minutes. The war began when Britain declared Zanzibar a protectorate of the British Empire. In 1893 the British installed their own 'puppet', Hamad Bin Thuwaini, into power to take care of the region. However, in 1896 he died suddenly and his cousin Khalid bin Barghash took his place, without British approval. Against British orders, Khalid refused to stand down and instead gathered his forces around the palace. The next day at 9am the order was given for British ships to begin bombarding the palace. Just two minutes later the palace's wooden structure collapsed with 3,000 defenders inside. The shelling ceased by 9.40am and with that the war ended.

Loch Ness never freezes. As we know, when the weather gets cold enough, lakes begin to freeze. However, this can't be said of the famous Loch Ness. Located in the Scottish Highlands, it has been known to experience temperatures as low as −15.2°C, but even in these conditions it never freezes. This is because of the loch's thermocline (the layer within a body of water where we see an abrupt change in temperature). Here, at approximately 30 metres deep, the water remains at 7°C. During the winter, the cooler surface water gets replaced by the rising warmer water from below. That may be the scientific explanation, but between you and me, we know the real reason is that Nessie likes her baths toasty.

Oxford University is older than the Aztec Empire.
Did you know that there is a university in the UK
that pre-dates the Aztec Empire? Oxford University,
renowned across the world, is actually older than the
Aztec Empire by roughly 230 years. It was established in
1096 AD during William II's reign.

The UK is full of accents. The UK is known for having a
multitude of accents all across the country. In total there
are roughly 56 different accents, even more than in the
USA, which has 42 accents despite having a total area
40 times bigger than that of the UK. It is estimated that
the British accent changes approximately every 25 miles.

The UK has the longest town name in Europe. The
longest town name in the UK doesn't just hold the record
in the UK, it also holds the record for the longest name
in Europe. Almost impossible for non-Welsh speakers to
say, Llanfairpwllgwyngyllgogerychwyrndrobwllllantysil-
iogogogoch has an impressive 58 letters. It may be the
longest place name in Europe, but it isn't the longest
in the entire world. That title goes to a hill on the North
Island of New Zealand, Taumatawhakatangihangakoau-
auotamateaturipukakapikimaungahoronukupokaiwhenu-
akitanatahu, which contains an impressive 85 letters.

USA

America consumes a lot of pizza. We know British people consume a staggering amount of tea every year, but what is the American version of this? Well, Americans eat about 100 acres of pizza every single day, which to put it into perspective is approximately 66 football pitches' worth.

America bought Alaska. Before becoming one of the 50 states of America, Alaska was owned by Russia during the nineteenth century. What's interesting, though, is that it was sold to the USA for roughly 2 cents per acre. You might be thinking 'absolute bargain', but given that Alaska is about 365,000,000 acres, this equated to $7.3 million, or £5.9 million.

The USA contains the largest lake in the world. Lake Superior is the largest freshwater lake in the world by surface area, and the third largest in terms of volume. It is so physically massive, at 31,700 square miles, that it stores enough water to cover all of America up to 0.3 metres deep. And by 'all of America', I mean both North *and* South America.

Unicorns might be real. Are unicorns real? That is a genuine question. They aren't, right? They are beautiful mythical creatures. Then why is it possible to get a unicorn hunting license from Michigan's Lake Superior State University?

Some lakes are deeper than you think. Thalassophobia is the fear of the ocean, and limnophobia is the fear of lakes – and that is exactly what you're about to have after reading this fact. Oregon's Crater Lake is 592 metres deep. That may not seem like a lot on paper, but consider this: it's deep enough to cover six Statues of Liberty stacked on top of each other.

The USA is home to the largest library in the world.
The biggest library in the world is located in Washington,
D.C. It has approximately 838 miles of bookshelves,
which if placed in a straight line end to end would be
long enough to stretch from Houston to Chicago.

The USA could have had a different name. We've
already learned about some interesting name changes
over the years in the USA, but I bet you've never heard
of this one. In 1893 there was a proposed amendment to
rename the country to the United States of Earth.

Utah is a happy place; Alabama not so much. Are you
a happy person or an unhappy person? Well, according
to research, that could depend on which state you live
in. Utah is supposedly the happiest state in the USA,
followed closely by Minnesota. However, both Alabama
and West Virginia rank as the unhappiest states.

There is a town with a population of one. Would you
ever live in a town entirely on your own? Well, for one
woman in the USA, this is her reality. Monowi, Nebraska
is the only officially incorporated town with a population
of one. The 81-year-old resident is the mayor, librarian
and bartender. This reminds me of *The Last of Us*. If you
know, you know.

You're more likely to be bitten by a human than a shark.
The likelihood of getting bitten by a human in New York is statistically higher than the likelihood of getting bitten by a shark off the coast of Florida. You are ten times more likely to get bitten by a New Yorker than by Jaws.

The USA has some famous firstborns. The vast majority of astronauts, US presidents and Nobel Prize winners were all firstborns in their families. For example, some names you may know are Barack Obama, George W. Bush, Bill Clinton, Jimmy Carter and Sally Ride. All of these famous people were in fact the firstborn of the family.

We will never finish painting the Golden Gate Bridge.
The Golden Gate Bridge is a never-ending paint job. Due to the saltwater that corrodes the paint, this magnificent structure has to be painted regularly. However, the corrosion happens at such a high rate that once the repainting of the bridge has been completed, another repainting job needs to start immediately.

Americans didn't always start their day with coffee.
Coffee wasn't always a popular way to start your day. The craze in the USA before the 1900s was to wash down a breakfast of plain porridge with a cup of beer or cider. This was even typical for children.

Your tweets might be in a library. Thanks to a collaboration with the social media platform Twitter, every public tweet sent in the USA has been digitally archived within the Library of Congress.

America lost an atomic bomb. Have you ever thought about going for a walk and discovering a lost atomic bomb? Well, that could be a possibility if you go to the USA, as in 1958 an atomic bomb disappeared from the arsenal of the United States Army, and to this day it has never been found. It was lost during a simulated combat mission in Georgia. The B-47 bomber carrying the weapon collided with an F-86. In an attempt to reduce weight, they were given the green light to jettison the bomb. It was dropped near the mouth of the Savannah River. Wherever it landed was its final resting place and it remains there to this very day.

OK, there's more than one lost atomic bomb. That's not the only time a nuclear bomb has been lost. I'm not entirely sure how humans manage to keep losing the most dangerous weapons ever created, but it has happened not once but on five other occasions. Thankfully most of them are in the depths of the ocean and not in someone's back garden.

There is an entire town in one house. Whittier is a city in the state of Alaska with a population of 217. Almost the entire population of this city lives in one building, which houses a school, a grocery store, a church and a hospital. The town has been nicknamed the 'town under one roof'.

California is bigger than Canada. If I were to ask you which is bigger, Canada or California, your answer would be Canada, right? Well, that may be true in terms of geographical size, but California wins when it comes to population.

Japan

Not all watermelons are round. One of my favourite facts about Japan is to do with fruit. We can all imagine that storing watermelons must be frustrating due to their shape, so the Japanese have come up with an efficient way to transport and store them. In order to keep his customers truly satisfied, one farmer found a way to grow square watermelons. This idea went viral and cubed watermelons have since been spotted in Russian markets for £690. And it doesn't end there – more recently, heart-shaped watermelons have emerged and continue to get rave reviews.

Tokyo is not the most expensive place to live.
Tokyo has a reputation around the world for being one of the most, if not *the* most expensive cities in the world to live in. However, according to the World Economic Forum, Tokyo no longer even makes the top ten. In fact according to WEF, as of 2022 Tokyo has moved down 24 places, now making it the 24th most expensive city to live in.

More Japanese people have a pet than a child. Many people choose to get a pet rather than have a child, but in Japan the statistics show a very clear preference for animal kind. Reports from 2012 show 21 million registered pets compared to 16.5 million children under the age of 15. This does have a negative effect, however, as it means Japan has one elderly person for every three citizens. If this trend continues, Japan will risk losing 40 per cent of its workforce.

Black cats aren't bad luck. In most places, if you are superstitious, you will probably want to lock yourself in a room if you see a black cat walking down the street — a black cat crossing your path is thought to be a sign of bad luck. However, this is not the case in Japan; the Japanese see black cats as a sign of good luck.

The numbers four and nine are bad luck. The reason for this cultural superstition is that the number four sounds like the word 'death' in Japanese, while the number nine sounds like the words 'suffering', 'agony' or 'torture'. The Japanese are so superstitious about these numbers that you are extremely unlikely to come across a fourth or a ninth floor in a high-rise building. Gifts should never be given in these quantities either. Other unfortunate numbers include 49, which sounds like 'to run over', and 24, which sounds like 'two deaths'.

You must slurp your noodles. If you dislike the sound of people eating, this will not be great for you. In Japan it is not considered rude to slurp your noodles, it is actually considered polite. Making loud slurping sounds means you're enjoying the food and you appreciate it.

You should give fruit as a dinner party gift. When invited to someone's house for dinner or a party in many parts of the world, bringing some form of alcoholic beverage seems like the safe way to go. But this cannot be said for Japan. If you don't know what to get your host in Japan, the safe option is fruit. The price of fruit in Japan can be astronomically high, which is why there is a 'fruit gifting shop' where some fruit can be as expensive as £22,000.

Japan has a long life expectancy. Japan has the second longest life expectancy in the world, after Monaco, at an average of 85 years old. In 2017 there were more than 2 million people living in Japan over the age of 90. The main factor behind their long lives is believed to be their high seafood intake, which consists of omega-3 fatty acids and carries a low risk of cancer, which is often linked to the consumption of red meats. It also helps that their healthcare system is one of the most accessible in the world, with the government covering 90 per cent of procedures.

Japan has vending machines for everything. We all love to grab a cheeky chocolate bar as a snack, but Japan has taken it to a whole new level. In fact, there are estimated to be 23 vending machines for every person in the country. That ratio is massive, considering that there are 125.44 million people living in Japan. It isn't just the number of vending machines that might surprise you, but what's in them too. Vending machines in Japan sell anything from cars to lettuce, underwear to hot ramen, and even eggs.

You can sleep at work. Have you ever had a late night before work, stayed up too late at the pub or, my excuse, got way too involved in a new Netflix series and just wanted to pass out at work the next day? Obviously you wouldn't do that because you would get fired. But in Japan sleeping on the job is not only OK, it actually has a name. *Inemuri* is the Japanese practice of sleeping at work. Taking a nap on the job is actually seen as a sign of dedication and hard work.

There is an underwater postbox. We all know checking our letterboxes can be a hassle and almost feel like a chore. Well, what if your letterbox wasn't just outside your house or at the end of your driveway but 10 metres underwater? There is an underwater postbox in Susami, Wakayama where divers leave water-resistant messages. You might be forgiven for thinking there isn't much post in an underwater postbox, but on a busy day it can receive up to 200 items.

Japanese game shows are TV gold. When you think of entertaining game shows you probably think of *Wheel of Fortune* or *Who Wants to Be a Millionaire?*. Well, Japan has managed to make game shows just that bit more interesting. How about watching a bunch of men dressed in latex suits climbing to the top of some super-slippery steps? Or what about a show where the contestants have to guess which objects are real and which are fake by taking a bite out of them?

Australia

Australia is the only 'continent nation'. Essentially this means that Australia is a continent as well as an independent country. On top of that, it is also the smallest, flattest and driest inhabited continent in the entire world.

A comedian tried to sell New Zealand. Did you know that there was an Australian comedian in 2006 by the name of Isaac Butterfield who put the country of New Zealand for sale on eBay? He started the bidding at AU$0.01, and before eBay closed the auction it had reached AU$3,000, or £1,610. Apparently the auction was a violation of eBay's policies.

The Australian dollar is very special. Speaking of Australian currency, the Australian dollar is considered to be one of the most advanced currencies in the world. It's not only waterproof, it's also made of polymer, making it notoriously hard to counterfeit.

Australia has a lot of beaches. For some, the idea of visiting every Australian beach sounds like a dream, but you would need to dedicate a lot of time to it. Australia has 10,685 beaches, meaning you'd have to visit one beach every day, of every week, of every month for 29 years to visit every single one.

Australians drink a lot of beer. As we know, Brits drink an unfathomable amount of tea and Americans eat a lot of pizza, but what about Aussies? As it turns out, Australia consumes 1.7 billion litres of beer per year. This equates to roughly 680 bottles of beer for each adult.

Australia has a perfect way of fighting crime. In 2013 Knox Council in Victoria decided to blast the classical music of Bach and Beethoven at different shopping centres at night to deter teenage loiterers.

There are a lot of venomous snakes. Many people are scared to visit Australia because of the wildlife that lives there. This fact isn't going to make that fear any better for you – of the 25 most venomous species of snake in the world, Australia is home to 21 of them.

There are loads of spiders too. You probably don't want to know this, but there are also over 1,500 species of spider happily waiting to be your next living nightmare in Australia.

Kangaroos outnumber humans. You probably already know that kangaroos are the national animal of Australia. In fact, there are over 34 million kangaroos in the country. There are so many that they considerably outnumber humans at only 25.67 million.

Kangaroos can't walk backwards. Kangaroos' inability to move backwards is used to symbolise a nation moving forwards.

Australia has a good minimum wage. From 1 July 2022, the minimum wage in Australia was AU$21.38 (or £11.48). In comparison, in Georgia, USA it is $5.15 (or £4.13), and in the UK it is £10.42.

Australia has a terrible mountain. Australia is home to a mountain called Mount Disappointment. The view from there is so disappointing that there was no better name for it.

The Sydney Opera House is a sphere. The Sydney Opera House is known around the world as an architectural wonder. However, you might not know that if you were to open out the sails of the Opera House and combine them, they would form a perfect sphere. This genius design came about when the architect was inspired while eating an orange.

We don't know about all the species that live in Australia. Australia is already home to species that are the stuff of absolute nightmares: snakes, spiders, need I go on? What makes matters worse is that there are so many different species in Australia that only 25 per cent of them are known to humans. That leaves 75 per cent that are as yet undiscovered.

The strangest war in human history

There have been many conflicts and wars over the years, but none quite like this one. I present to you the Great Emu War of 1932. At this time, the Great Depression led Australia to declare war on a flightless bird, the emu. Bizarrely, the country actually lost a full-scale war against the birds.

The war began when the Australian government attempted to launch a soldier settlement programme to help veterans of World War I. The policy compensated 5,000 soldiers with huge areas of farmland for cultivating wheat, and it gave the soldiers their lives

back. However, this farmland was located in western Australia, one of the most remote and inhospitable places in the country, known as emu country. Just seven years after the farms were given out, emus began to devastate them. It wasn't long before the government reclassified this flightless bird from a protected species to vermin, and with that the war began.

Over 20,000 emus were confirmed to be destroying the farmlands and eating crops grown by the soldiers. The first battle of the Great Emu War saw soldiers armed with 10,000 rounds of ammunition and machine guns launch an open attack in Perth – which failed. It was reported that the birds were too quick and too tough to kill. In fact, nearly all the emus escaped. Even after several days of war, the emus appeared to be flocking back in greater numbers, almost seeming to have a 'strategy' of their own. On 10 December 1932, the army was asked to call off the Great Emu War. Instead, the government opted to provide the farmers with free ammunition and incentivised them to kill the emus themselves over time by placing bounties on them.

The real question is, how did humans lose a war to birds? We will go more into depth about emus later in the animal section and I will tell you exactly how they won.

Africa

Africa is the second largest continent in the world.
Africa is so large that it has between 1,500 and 2,000
spoken languages, each with different dialects. The
top four languages most widely spoken on the African
continent are Arabic, English, Swahili and French.

Africa exists in all four hemispheres. It is hard to
grasp the true size of the continent of Africa as it
covers nearly 12 million square miles. As a result,
it is the only continent that spreads across all four
hemispheres. The vast majority of the continent can
be found within the eastern hemisphere and a small
portion in the western hemisphere. Two-thirds is
located in the northern hemisphere and one-third lies
in the southern hemisphere.

The first heart transplant happened in Africa. Africa
is home to the surgeon who performed the world's first
human-to-human heart transplant operation. Christiaan
Neethling Barnard was a South African cardiac surgeon
who completed the surgery on 3 December 1967.

The oldest university in the world is in Africa.
We have previously spoken about the fact that Oxford University pre-dates the Aztec Empire; however, it is not the oldest university in the world. That honour goes to the University of Karueein, which is the oldest existing and continually operating educational institute on the planet. The university was founded in AD 859 by Fatima al-Fihri in Fez.

Africa used to have a different name. We know this massive continent as Africa, but this is not always what it was called. Experts have said that the original ancient name of Africa was 'Alkebulan'. The name translates to 'mother of mankind', but some sources suggest it translates to 'the garden of Eden'. The word 'Alkebulan' is extremely old and its origins are indigenous.

CHAPTER 5:

The

HUMAN BODY

£36,000,000

You might think
that you're not that
interesting. However, I
would personally argue
that humans might just
be the most fascinating
things to ever exist.
I am about to take you
down a rabbit hole ...
of your own body.

General facts

We might not really be alive. Now, try not to overthink this one, but the human body is made up of atoms like hydrogen, carbon, nitrogen and oxygen. However, atoms are technically not living things. That means that if we were to pick ourselves apart, one atom at a time, we would arrive at an amount of atomic dust that had never been alive, yet all of which had once been you.

You can't actually touch anything. Everything – you, me, a chair, this book – is made of atoms. Atoms contain electrons and these electrons repel each other. What we call 'touching' is actually our brain interpreting the electromagnetic force between atoms. This is known as 'electron repulsion'. Electrons are negatively charged, so when they get too close they will push each other away. That means that when you sit on a chair, you're not actually sitting on the chair. What's even more disturbing is that physics dictates that if two particles were actually to touch, it would create a nuclear reaction.

You're not the same person you used to be. Did you know that your skin renews itself every 28 days? Every year an average human sheds four kilograms of skin. Specifically, I am referring to the thin outer layer of your skin, known as the epidermis, which is in fact loaded with dead skin cells.

Blood

You are part gold. Human blood contains metal atoms such as iron, chromium, manganese, zinc, lead and copper. You might be surprised to learn that your blood also contains gold. Granted, you aren't going to become the next Bill Gates thanks to the gold in your blood, but your body does contain about 0.2 milligrams of the stuff.

Blood types vary by country. I bet at some point in your life you have been curious about your blood type. Well, blood types vary to a certain extent by population. The most common blood type in the USA is O positive and the least common is AB negative. The most common blood type in Japan is A positive. According to the NHS, the most common blood group is 'O', as almost half of the UK population (48 per cent) resides within this group.

Your blood is heavy. Did you know that the average adult human body contains approximately 1.2–1.5 gallons of blood? Blood makes up approximately 10 per cent of a person's total body weight.

Blood vessels are very long. The body of a human child contains 60,000 miles of blood vessels – this is long enough to circle the globe more than twice, or to reach one-quarter of the distance to the moon. In an adult, all the blood vessels laid end to end would stretch approximately 100,000 miles.

Human blood is red for a reason. What determines the colour of blood? It actually depends on the type of respiratory pigment used to transport oxygen to cells via the circulatory system. The respiratory pigment in humans is a protein known as haemoglobin, which is found in red blood cells.

Your body

You are truly worth a lot. Many people are fixated on making as much money as they possibly can. Well, I have either the easiest or the hardest way for you to make your millions (I'll let you decide which). All of the parts of the human body are worth a lot of money. In fact, the entire body, including all the organs, bones, ligaments, etc., could fetch a grand total of £36 million. Granted, we don't know whether the selling of one's own body parts is often done by individuals, but there are places like the black market and the dark web where body parts of human beings have been sold.

We develop from a bumhole. When a human embryo cell begins to develop, you might be surprised to learn that the anus develops first. To give a little bit more explanation, humans belong to a subclassification of species called 'deuterostomes'. When the embryo begins to develop, these deuterostomes form a mouth known as a 'blastospore'. However, this 'mouth' ultimately becomes your anus. No real way of sugarcoating that one.

Belly buttons are filthy. Growing up, we were taught to clean our teeth, our ears and wash our hands, but were you ever told to clean your belly button? Well, I hope you were, and here's why. The average belly button is filled with many forms of bacteria; specifically, there are on average 67 different bacteria species living and thriving inside your unwashed belly button.

You glow in the dark. Bioluminescence is a natural phenomenon in which living creatures emit a certain level of light, and humans are actually on that list. Chemical energy within the human body gets converted into light energy, and research suggests that you are at your 'brightest' at around 4pm. The only reason we cannot see this light with our naked eye is that the glow is a thousand times weaker than what we can see with our eyes.

Your stomach gets nervous too. When you get nervous or embarrassed, a natural response is for blood to rush to the skin on your face, causing you to blush. However, this isn't the only area where this happens – at the same time as you're blushing on the surface, your stomach lining is blushing too.

Your nose is wild. How many scents can your nose detect? Try and give a rough answer. Well, unless you guessed about 1 trillion, you would be wrong. A 2004 study published in *Science* found that humans have the ability to detect 1 trillion different individual scents. However, in the same study it was suggested that more research needed to be carried out as that number could be significantly higher.

We might have a sixth sense. We have been told that humans have five senses: sight, hearing, taste, smell and touch. However, it has also been noted that humans have other senses, such as proprioception, which is the sense of where your body is in space.

You shed more than a snake. Humans shed a lot more than you might think. In fact, we shed approximately 600,000 particles of skin every single hour, which equates to 0.7 kilograms in a year, so by the age of 70 you will have shed 49 kilograms of skin in your lifetime.

You had eyes before you had eyelids. During a human's development, at the seven-week mark, the main parts of the eye, including the cornea, pupil, iris, retina and lens, begin to develop. However, it isn't until ten weeks that a foetus forms eyelids. This means there is a point where the developing foetus is blankly staring at nothing for at least a week.

CHAPTER 6:

HISTORY

We all remember history in school, and before you think this is just another one of those lessons, think again. Here are the most insane facts and events that happened throughout history that were most likely never in your history books.

General facts

You won't believe who designed the US flag.
The current US flag was designed in 1958 by a 17-year-old as part of a school project.

There have been some controversial Nobel Peace Prize nominations. Hitler, Mussolini and Stalin were all nominated for the Nobel Peace Prize.

The Pope once declared war on cats. Granted, I am a dog person, but I don't think I would go as far as Pope Gregory, the leader of the Catholic Church, who between the years 1233 and 1234 declared a war on cats. He stated that 'black cats are an instrument of Satan' and ordered them to be exterminated throughout Europe. As the famous saying goes, what goes around comes around, and due to the drastic decrease in the population of cats, the number of plague-carrying rats spiked, and the devastation caused by the plague was worse than it would have been had the war on cats never begun.

Some surprising people were alive at the same time.
I know this one will be hard to comprehend, but Picasso
was alive at the same time as Eminem and Charles
Darwin. I will let that sink in for a second. Here are the
dates if you don't believe me: Darwin was alive from
1809 to 1882, Picasso was alive from 1881 to 1973 and
Eminem was born in 1972 and is still alive today.

**Two more surprising people had overlapping
lives.** Those aren't the only people you might have
thought lived in two completely different time periods.
Shakespeare and Pocahontas were alive at the same
time too.

You could have had spider webs in your first aid kit.
Spider webs were used as bandages in ancient times.
Specifically, in ancient Greece and Rome, doctors used
spider webs to make bandages for their patients. It was
thought that spider webs contained natural antiseptic and
anti-fungal properties, preventing any future infection.

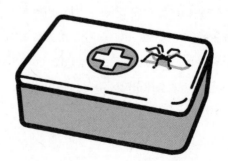

You could also have had mouldy bread in your first aid kit. It doesn't stop there. Going back to ancient Egypt, mouldy bread was actually used to treat wounds. It was believed that the bacteria within the mould would act as an antibiotic and heal the cut or wound.

You drink dinosaur urine every single day. The average Brit drinks three to four cups of water a day. Although that seems like a lot, humans haven't been on this planet for long enough to have used most of Earth's water. Dinosaurs, on the other hand, walked this planet for 186 million years, which gave them a lot of time to consume the planet's water. In fact, it is estimated that every time you buy water from a shop or pour yourself some from a tap, it is almost certain that that water once passed through a dinosaur. Yes, that's right — water, the substance we need to survive, is dinosaur pee.

Tanks were designed to make tea. As a Brit myself, I would agree that there are few things as good as a warm cup of tea on a cold evening, but I'm not sure I would have gone this far. During World War II British soldiers kept stopping to take tea breaks as they would get famished in battle. So, since 1945, tanks have doubled as tea-making facilities.

Christmas was banned in Britain. What are the two times of year we all get excited about? Surely it's summer and Christmas. But what if I told you that one of these was once banned in Britain? That's right, between the years of 1644 and 1660, Lord Protector Oliver Cromwell actually banned any celebration of Christmas. He was a very strict Christian and he believed that fun activities like dancing, music and even make-up upset God. The English were less than pleased with this decision and there were riots. Scotland, on the other hand, was not bothered and Christmas didn't become a public holiday until 1958.

An emperor declared war on the ocean. War and conflict aren't usually fun topics, but this might be the one exception. During the Roman era, when Emperor Caligula was in power, he declared war on the sea. That's right, the actual ocean – or more specifically on Neptune, the god of the sea. He lined up his soldiers and artillery on the beach and ordered them to 'whip the waves' and stab the sea with their swords and spears. Of course, after this undeniable victory, he couldn't go home empty-handed, so he commanded his men to collect shells from the beach as 'war booty'.

India hid a wonder of the world. We dream about visiting the many wonders on this beautiful and fascinating planet, but during World War II one of these wonders would have looked completely unrecognisable, thanks to some brilliant strategy. The Taj Mahal rightfully claims a spot among the Seven Wonders of the World for obvious reasons. However, during World War II, when bombings were frequent, India wanted to keep this building safe from bombings because it knew that, as a landmark, it would have a target on its back. To keep the 73-metre-tall building hidden, it was covered in bamboo. From the air it appeared to be just a bamboo stockpile. It actually worked, and no enemy bombers realised what was really hidden beneath.

The Ancient Greeks punished their politicians. Poor political decisions don't only happen nowadays; in ancient Greece there were significant punishments for being a bad politician. The Ancient Greeks, if they saw fit, could vote to have a politician banished from the city of Athens for up to ten years. This was done in an effort to prevent the 'corrupt' politician from slowly taking over. I wonder if people believe that way of thinking should be brought back today?

Napoleon was defeated by 3,000 rabbits. The famous quote 'don't judge me by my wins, judge me by my losses' is very humbling for some, and straight-up embarrassing for one historic military leader, Napoleon Bonaparte. One of the greatest and most unforgettable defeats of his long career was by 3,000 very angry rabbits. In July 1807, after the successful ending of the conflict between Russia and France, Napoleon asked his chief of staff to organise a rabbit hunt. Three thousand rabbits were collected so they could be released

and later hunted, but rather than finding wild rabbits (because let's be honest, who has time for that?), the chief of staff decided to buy domesticated ones. On top of that, Napoleon happened to slightly resemble the man who was in charge of feeding the rabbits, and since they had been locked in a cage all day with no food, the moment they were released, they didn't run off as Napoleon had anticipated but charged straight at him. It took a while for others to assist Napoleon, and it was only when they realised he was in actual danger that they intervened. After much swatting, Napoleon did escape the rabbits' furry clutches.

World War II was the backdrop to a great love story.
After hundreds of mind-boggling facts, I'm excited to share this first wholesome one with you. Hundreds of love letters between two gay World War II soldiers are being made into a book. These letters actually contain the sentence: 'Wouldn't it be wonderful if all our letters could be published in the future in a more enlightened time? Then all the world could see how in love we are.' During military training, a soldier by the name of Gilbert Bradley exchanged hundreds of letters with his sweetheart, who signed their letters with the initial 'G'. It was more than 70 years later that it was discovered 'G' stood for Gordon.

A bear almost caused World War III. We all hope that World War III will never come to fruition. However, there was a point in history when, thanks to a black bear and a faulty switch, it almost became all too real. On 25 October 1962, a guard at the Duluth Sector Direction Center noticed a shadowy figure attempting to climb the facility's perimeter. He shot at it and raised the alarm to every air base in the vicinity, assuming it was part of a wider Soviet attack. However, it did not end there. At a nearby base someone flicked the wrong switch, so instead of sending a standard security warning, an emergency siren told pilots to scramble and take to the skies with fully armed nuclear weapons. Everyone was on edge, believing the strike to be connected to the then ongoing Cuban Missile Crisis, but thankfully in the end the base commander figured out what was going on and intercepted the pilots by driving a truck onto the runway as they started their engines. World War III was over before it began.

One man might have prevented the *Titanic* disaster. We all know the tragic story of the *Titanic*, but did you know that there was one person who, had they boarded the ship, could have prevented the disaster? David Blair was supposed to be the second officer on the *Titanic*, but at the very last minute he was

reassigned to a different ship. On 9 April 1912, while in a rush to leave the ship, David Blair accidentally took the key for the crow's nest telephone with him and stowed the lookouts' binoculars in what would have been his cabin. It was later mentioned to the American inquiry that they were unable to find them during the voyage. Of course, we'll never know whether the fate of the *Titanic* would have been different had the lookouts been in possession of the binoculars, but it does make you wonder.

The Egyptians had birth control. This is going to make a lot of people cringe, but here we go. The Egyptians had a very specific 'recipe' for birth control, which involved two ingredients: crocodile poo and honey. Mixing these two ingredients together would give you a form of pessary, a block that could be inserted as a contraceptive.

People also used heavy metals as birth control.
It doesn't stop there – all across the world ancient
civilisations used heavy metals as a form of birth control.
These included mercury, lead and arsenic. Ancient
Egyptian, Assyrian and Greek women would also have
drunk liquid mercury. What makes it worse is that these
poisonous substances could cause both lung and kidney
failure, as well as possible brain damage. And in case
you were wondering, they did not work as birth control.

AD 536 was the worst year to be alive. We have
spoken about the most boring day ever, but have you
ever wondered what was the worst year in human
history? Your mind may jump to the Black Death or the
Great Depression, one of the world wars, or even more
recently, 2020. However, they would all be wrong – the
worst year in human history was AD 536, also known
as 'the year of darkness'. For a year and a half the sun
was completely covered by a thick fog. The most widely
accepted explanation for this is that the fog was caused
by a volcanic eruption in Iceland, which led to a volcanic
winter and the coldest decade in the past 2,300 years.
This led to mass crop failure, which in turn caused mass
starvation. It wasn't long afterwards that the bubonic
plague began to circulate across Europe. And that's why
historians have dubbed this the worst year to be alive.

Never complain about having a headache during ancient times. No one in the present day particularly enjoys the prospect of visiting a doctor, but in ancient civilisations this was less of an annoyance and more of a living nightmare. One of the worst things you could do would be to tell a doctor that you had a headache. The solution to this was to drill a hole in the side of your head to release the demons.

Ancient dentists were no better. Arguably the dentist was even worse than the doctor. You'd better have hoped you didn't have anything wrong with your teeth, otherwise you would have had to visit the 'Tooth Man'. This person would travel with musicians, not as a way to calm the patient as they had a peaceful check-up, but to drown out the screams of the patients.

The elites never used to get away with crimes. Aztec society had a very interesting set of rules, which many could argue have been abandoned in the modern day. In fact, crimes that were committed by nobles were very often punished more severely than those committed by commoners. This is because as an 'elite' member of society the criminal would have been held to significantly higher standards and been expected to behave better as an example to the commoners.

Decisions used to be made drunk and sober.
A hilarious concept was created by the Ancient
Persians when it came to debating important ideas:
it was done first while sober and then again while
drunk. This came from the belief that an idea had to
sound good in both states of mind to be considered
acceptable.

Vicious Vikings

Vikings are not what you imagine. If I told you to picture a Viking, you would probably think of a large person wearing armour and a horned helmet. Well, what if I told you that every Viking fancy dress costume you have ever seen is historically inaccurate? Vikings did not wear horned helmets. Of course, they wore headgear into battle, but they would have been simple helmets made of iron or leather; horns would have been impractical. This specific depiction of Vikings dates back to opera in the 1800s when costume designers created horned helmets for the Viking characters, and from there the stereotype was born.

The Vikings abandoned their sick children. Vikings relied upon strength, so if a child was born with a disability or sickness, they would be abandoned. This horrendous way of life came about because the Vikings believed that a sick child could not contribute to society, so they would be left alone in the wilderness or thrown into the sea.

The days of the week are named after Viking gods. Have you ever stopped to consider why humans named the days of the week Monday, Tuesday, Wednesday, Thursday, Friday, Saturday and Sunday? As it turns out, the days of the week are named after gods worshipped by the Vikings:

Monday (Manadagr). The Nordic days of the week that we still use today start with the moon and end with the sun. The moon gives us Monday, named after Mani, the personification of the moon in Norse mythology.

Tuesday (Tysdagr). The second day of the week is named after the Norse god Tyr. Old English translates Tyr as Tiw, so Anglo-Saxons dubbed this day 'Tiwesdaeg', which eventually led to the modern spelling of Tuesday.

Wednesday (Odinsdagr). This day of the week is known as Woden's day, which is the Old English version of Odin.

Thursday (Thorsdagr). Thursday is Thor's day. The god of thunder is the Norse counterpart of the Roman deity Jupiter.

Friday (Frjardagr). Many scholars debate as to which Norse god Friday is named after. However, a general consensus is that it was named after the goddess Frigg, wife of Odin.

Saturday (Laugardagr). Saturday is named after the Roman god Saturn. In Old Norse, *dagr* means 'day' and *Laugar* means 'hot water'. The Norse version of Saturday makes sense, then, as these days of the week were partly influenced by Christianity, and since Sunday is the Sabbath, it was common for people to bathe the day before they went to church.

Sunday (Sunnudagr). Sunday was named after Sol, the personification of the sun in the Norse and Roman myths.

Ancient Romans

The Romans washed their clothes with urine.
There are many different companies that make products for us to wash our clothes in the modern day, but the Romans had a solution that was a lot closer to home – I mean, a *lot* closer. They were convinced that the ammonia found in urine could break apart the dirt on their clothes. Ammonia is known to be a powerful bleaching agent. However, I wouldn't try this at home.

A Roman would swap your tooth-whitening toothpaste for urine. This is not the end of the uses of urine, as it was also used for whitening Romans' teeth. Urine contains nitrogen and phosphorus, so it was used to help grow fruit; evidently it worked well, especially for pomegranates. As well as being used for laundry and fertiliser, it was also used to heal sick animals. The Romans believed that urine held the power to cure animals and would force them to drink human urine. You should be thankful that we have better products and medicines for all these needs in modern times.

Roman toilets were terrible. Going to the toilet may be one of the few moments of peace and quiet you experience in a busy day, but if you lived in Roman society this would have been far from the truth. In fact, there was a very real risk that when you entered the toilet you might die. There was a plethora of creatures living in the sewage system in Rome, and they could crawl up and bite people while they were ... sitting. Worse than that, though, was the methane build-up, which would sometimes get so bad that it could ignite and explode underneath you. I may have just given you an irrational fear of your own toilet, and for that I apologise.

Roman gladiators had a skin routine. Roman gladiators weren't just used for their blood. Women were known to rub the dead skin cells of gladiators on their faces. During these times soap was a luxury item and rather difficult to come by, so athletes would clean themselves by covering their bodies in oil and scraping off the dead skin cells with a tool known as a 'strigil'. Now, typically, dead skin cells come off you and that's the end of the story, but that was not the case if you were a gladiator. Your sweat and skin scrapings were put into a bottle and sold to women as an aphrodisiac, in the hope that the dead skin cells of a gladiator would make the woman irresistible to men.

Gladiator blood was used as medicine. As we're quickly establishing, the past wasn't a great time to have any doctor-related needs. However, we're yet to explore one of the strangest facts: gladiator blood was used as medicine. This revelation comes from multiple Roman authors, who reported that the blood of dead gladiators was collected and sold as medicine. Were the sellers early entrepreneurs? It was believed that gladiator blood had the power to cure epilepsy, so many would drink it. Others weren't quite as 'civilised'. Rather than drinking the blood, others would rip out the gladiators' livers and eat them raw. So how did people get their daily dose of blood when Rome banned gladiatorial combat? As it turns out, they kept their 'treatments' going by drinking the blood of decapitated prisoners.

The Romans had an energy drink I will not be purchasing. Charioteers drank an energy drink made of goat dung. They either boiled goat dung in vinegar or ground it into a powder and mixed it into other drinks. Apparently this gave them a little boost when they were exhausted. This wasn't an energy drink created for poor people – Emperor Nero himself loved the kick of a goat-dung energy drink.

Goat dung was used as a medicine too. Back in Roman times, if you got a minor injury, you couldn't just run to the cabinet for a plaster. No, they had other solutions – Romans would patch up their wounds with goat dung. The best goat dung, according to Pliny the Elder, was collected during the spring.

Owls were bad omens. In Roman times, owls were considered to be bad omens, a little like our superstitions involving black cats today. They had other superstitions too: the scent of cyclamen flowers was thought to prevent baldness, ringing bells would ease the pain of childbirth and seeing bees was a sign of good luck.

Roman generals had a bad time if their army lost a battle. Being a Roman general, although a massive honour, was a terrifying prospect. All I have to say is you'd better make sure you won your battles. Generals were safely positioned behind the army while the fighting took place, but if the battle was lost it would very much fall back into the general's hands. In fact, the general had two options: to kill themselves or join the next army for what would essentially be a fight to the death.

The Romans were superstitious. The Romans had their own superstitions. A popular one was that they feared literally anything having to do with the 'left'. This was reflected in the word they used for 'left', which was *sinister*. If you were unfortunate enough to be left-handed, you would be referred to as *sinistra*.

Being late was no big deal. Now this one I could probably get behind. For ancient Romans, being late was never a big deal. This was most likely because they didn't have watches. In fact, they would rely on the sun to determine what time it was. I can imagine on a cloudy day it was almost guaranteed you would be late.

The sewers had a goddess. The Cloaca Maxima was Rome's famous sewer system. It was very popular and one of the marvels of the ancient world; it was well ahead of its time. This is where the goddess enters the story. As we know, the Romans had a lot of gods. They had a god for pretty much everything, including Cloacina, the goddess who protected Rome's sewers. As well as protecting the sewers, Cloacina had another responsibility: to purify sexual intercourse in marriage.

The Romans ate meals lying down. The Romans didn't eat their meals sitting on a chair at a table. If they were invited to someone's house for dinner, they would find a row of couches to lie down on with a big table in the middle.

Roman food

I am now going to take you on a little culinary journey through the five-star meals of Roman society.

Garum was a sauce that the Romans would put on just about everything they ate, but it was quite unlike the tomato ketchup we use so liberally today. Garum was made using fish intestines and blood left to marinate in the hot sun for several weeks as it fermented. Once this process was complete, several herbs were added and it was ready to be served alongside the main dish. But what were the main dishes?

Giraffe meat was very popular. Nowadays we think of giraffes as relatively peaceful animals, but in Roman times they would have been used in gladiator fights. Research suggests that, post-fight, the slaughtered long-necked animals would have been served as a main dish.

Next up we have jellyfish, which was reserved only for the wealthy in Rome. The best-preserved Roman cookery book, the *Apicius*, describes the consumption of jellyfish.

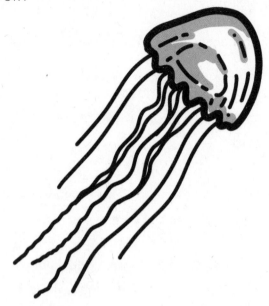

How exactly would you prepare and eat a jellyfish, you may ask? Well, the Romans enjoyed a jellyfish omelette.

We aren't done with weird sea creatures, because the Romans also ate sea urchins. I don't suppose we're in a position to judge when we enjoy crabs, shrimp and oysters! Much like jellyfish, sea urchins were reserved for the wealthy in Rome.

We often consider rodents to be disgusting, disease-carrying creatures, but in ancient Rome dormice were seen as a delicacy, as well as a status symbol. In fact, as a way of showing off their wealth, wealthy Romans would actually weigh the rodents in front of their guests before cooking them.

When we consider the parts of an animal we consume, we don't often think about the tongue. I'm fairly sure you'd avoid the tongue of a flamingo, but this was another strange status symbol in ancient Rome. Apparently if you owned a lot of these birds, you were known to be rich, and your prestige in the eyes of Rome only increased if you sacrificed one of those birds to eat. The tongue was especially enjoyable with some garum on the side.

Ancient Egyptians

The Egyptians invented toothpaste. We have the Egyptians to thank for a couple of things, but I would say the biggest is the invention of toothpaste. There were no dentists during those times, yet they still contributed to innovations in dental hygiene. However, the ingredients in early toothpaste were questionable: powdered ox hooves, ashes, burned eggshells and pumice.

The Egyptians were buried with toothpicks. The Egyptians even cared about dental hygiene in the afterlife. Mummies were buried with toothpicks in the belief that they would need them to get food out from between their teeth in the afterlife.

The Egyptians gave up their eyebrows for their cat. Are you a cat or a dog person? All I'm going to say is, it was better to be a dog person in ancient Egypt if you cared about your eyebrows. If someone's cat died, it was mummified, and as a sign of mourning and respect from the owners, they would shave off their eyebrows and continue to mourn the loss of the cat until their eyebrows grew back.

You could be punished for harming a cat. Cats were highly respected animals during this time, so much so that Egypt still has many statues and paintings of every type of feline. If you were to kill a cat in ancient Egypt, even by accident, you could be sentenced to death. This is because Egyptian mythology portrayed gods and goddesses as having the power to transform themselves into different animals. The deity that could transform into a cat was Bastet.

The Egyptians predicted the future through poo. Have you ever had your future told, maybe by a psychic or a palm reader? I'm going to guess that some of you have. But have you ever had your future read by someone analysing your poo? I present to you 'scatomancy', a very popular way of predicting the future in ancient Egypt. This process involved analysing someone's droppings to determine their future.

The workers were paid in radishes. In today's society, we work to earn money, but this was not always the case. In ancient Egypt, radishes, onions and garlic were given as wages to workers because they provided workers with a way to fight infectious diseases.

The Egyptians had pregnancy tests. Ancient Egyptians also had a very particular way of determining if someone was pregnant and it was surprisingly accurate, with a 70 per cent prediction rate. A woman who was thought to be pregnant would urinate on seeds. If the seeds sprouted, it was a sign that she might be pregnant.

The Egyptians had the worst punishment. Disrespecting a culture's god has different consequences across the world, but in ancient Egypt they were unique. During these times violent crimes were relatively rare, and the most awful crimes were often considered to involve showing disrespect towards the Sun God. Vandalising or robbing a temple would result in the worst form of execution: you would be burned alive. The Ancient Egyptians believed that you needed to preserve the physical body after death, and if you destroyed the body, it would leave the person with no vessel in the afterlife, essentially causing them to continue to suffer after death.

People used mummy bandages as food wrappers.
There was once an outbreak of cholera that was linked
to wrapping food in paper made from old mummy
bandages. In the early 1900s ancient Egypt was popular
around the world, so much so that mummies were
often imported to Europe to be unwrapped during
parties. Unfortunately, respect for mummies was low
and old mummy bandages were often cheaper than
actual paper. An American businessman saw this as an
opportunity; he decided that he would save a bit of cash
by wrapping food in imported old, brown mummy paper.
It wasn't long afterwards that people began to catch
cholera and the outbreak was eventually linked back to
this money-saving idea.

People used to eat mummies. During the 1600s and
1700s in Europe, a craze swept the continent where
people crushed up bits of human and ate them in
order to cure themselves of various ailments. This
craze is believed to have begun with people crushing
up mummies and putting them in tinctures, and this
gradually developed into people drinking blood to cure
blood-related illnesses, as well as eating bits of crushed
skull to deal with problems with the brain.

The pyramids once looked very different. The pyramids were originally paper white and smooth as glass. At the very top of each pyramid was a golden capstone that gleamed in the desert sun. These coverings have fallen off over time, either due to earthquakes or because they were cut off and taken away.

CHAPTER 7:

ANIMALS

When you look at the animal kingdom through pictures and videos online, or even safari tours on holiday, you probably think, *Wow*. You most likely smile as you watch a dolphin peek above the water, or a penguin waddling on the ice. Well, this chapter may just have you looking at the animal kingdom in a different light.

General facts

There is an immortal animal. Humans have been searching for the secret of immortality for many generations, but there is one species that has beaten us to it. A species of jellyfish known as *Turritopsis dohrnii* is considered to be immortal due to its response to physical damage. It has the ability to revert in its development process to being a polyp when it gets old or injured, essentially restarting its life from scratch.

Dogs have scary secrets. Have you ever wondered why dogs love squeaky toys so much? It reminds them of their natural urge to hunt and the sound of scared or injured prey.

Lions are wholesome. Just as our parents encourage us when we are young and build up our confidence, adult lions do the same with their offspring. They will pretend to be hurt when their young bite them in order to encourage them to feel strong.

Butterflies eat you. Butterflies seem cute, but keep this in mind next time one lands on you and you get all happy thinking you've made a new friend: butterflies' tastebuds are in their feet. They are attracted to the salt in your sweat – a very common substance in their diet. When they land on you, they are just having a midday snack. They have about as much emotional connection to you as the McDonalds you visited last week.

Dolphins bully stingrays. Some animals that we deem adorable are actually the animal version of Satan. Take dolphins, for example. You know how you enjoy trying to skim a stone across the water when you go to the lake or the beach? Well, funnily enough, dolphins enjoy that too, but instead of stones they use stingrays. A dolphin will swim down, catch one, bring it to the surface and skim it like a stone.

Sperm whales are loud. Sperm whales are the loudest mammals on the planet, with their vocalisations reaching 230 decibels. To put this into perspective, stand too close to a sound this loud and it could vibrate you to death by causing an air bubble in your brain.

A cat was made the mayor of a town. As I've said, I'm a dog person, but this fact is really something. The Alaskan town of Talkeetna has a population of 772, and in 2000 they appointed an orange cat by the name of Stubbs as honorary mayor. Stubbs remained in office for 20 years.

Penguins are a menace. Next time you watch *Blue Planet*, you're going to look at the penguins – specifically the emperor penguin – differently. If an emperor penguin loses its child, rather than making another bundle of joy, it will go and take another penguin's young to raise it as its own. Mind you, it's also common for emperor penguins to get bored and abandon the stolen babies. Talk about a troubled childhood.

A penguin was knighted. Did you know that there was a penguin in Norway that was knighted? This legendary penguin goes by the name of Sir Nils Olav III. Nils was given the role of mascot to the Norwegian Guard and very quickly moved up the ranks.

Penguins propose to each other. Penguins truly are interesting birds, but did you know there is a species of penguin, the gentoo penguin, that proposes with a pebble? That's right, they are known to collect a stone and drop it at the feet of a potential mate. If she is impressed by the presentation of the pebble, the pair may go on to build a nest out of pebbles and begin their life together. Generally, penguins are loyal to their spouses, with studies showing that 89 per cent of Galapagos penguins stick with their mates. However, another study in 1999 showed only 15 per cent of emperor penguins seek out the same partner each breeding season. The fidelity rate of penguins consistently returning to the same partner is between 59 per cent and 89 per cent, but let's be honest, that's still higher than most human beings.

Dolphins have an evil side. Before you read this book, you might have been forgiven for thinking dolphins were cute creatures who do no harm, but not only do they skim stingrays, they also kill for sport. People on Scotland's east coast began to notice baby porpoises with 'horrifying internal injuries' washing up dead on the beaches. Dolphins were caught on film using a technique known as echolocation to cause internal damage to and even kill the baby porpoises.

Pandas are the worst animal parent. Dolphins aren't the only creature competing for the crown of incredibly cute yet completely evil – pandas are in the running too. Typically pandas give birth to twins, but they aren't very happy about that and they only want one baby, so they pick the weaker of the two and ignore them in favour of the stronger sibling.

We are similar to elephants. Have you ever looked at an elephant and thought, *Yeah, we are the same*? Probably not, right? Well, what if I told you that you are more similar to an elephant than you think? Elephants are the only other animals to have chins. They also have a sense of self, show empathy, are curious and are able to develop behaviour through learning and mimicry. In addition, they understand the importance of teamwork and, similar to humans, they grieve for their loved ones.

There are more ants than humans. What I am about to write sounds like the plot of an apocalypse movie rather than reality: for every human on earth there are estimated to be 2.5 million ants. Ants have the ability to carry between 10 and 50 times their own body weight, so here's the apocalypse part: if ants developed similar brain power to that of humans, using a coordinated attack and their hive mind they could completely destroy humanity and take over earth for themselves.

It wouldn't take many ants to cover your entire body. There might be 2.5 million ants per person on the planet, but it only takes 3,000 of them to cover the average human body. That's a fact to make your skin crawl.

Blood isn't always red. When we think of different coloured blood, our thoughts probably go to alien TV shows and movies. Well, what if I told you the full colour spectrum of blood is actually a lot closer to home? Animals such as crustaceans, spiders, squid, octopuses and some arthropods have blue-coloured blood. Some worms and leeches have green blood, while many marine species of worms have violet blood. Sometimes it isn't always so vibrant: insects like beetles and butterflies have colourless or pale-yellow blood.

Colourful but deadly

When it comes to nature, the more vibrant and colourful the animal, the deadlier it is. You might want to keep your distance if you spot any of these creatures in the wild; they could be the end of you:

The poison dart frog. The poison dart frog comes in a range of colours, including yellows, reds and oranges, greens and blues, but don't be fooled by their vibrant beauty. Just one touch can send you to meet your ancestors in minutes. Poison dart frogs release a potent toxin that is secreted from their skin, which is so deadly that indigenous peoples in South and Central America use it to poison the tips of their blow darts. If you are still in any doubt about the danger these colourful frogs pose, the most lethal of all is the golden poison frog, which carries enough toxin to kill 10–20 men. All that devastation can be caused by a creature just four centimetres long.

The blue-ringed octopus. You might have seen a viral TikTok of a woman unknowingly picking up one of the most dangerous creatures on the planet – a blue-ringed octopus – and thinking it was cute. (She was fortunately fine, by the way.) The blue-ringed octopus takes the title of most venomous creature, but what makes it worse is that currently no antivenom exists. I would say to be wary, but this octopus's bite is thought to be completely painless, so until the respiratory distress and paralysis kick in, you'll think it was just a normal day on the beach.

The flamboyant cuttlefish. The flamboyant cuttlefish is definitely a unique-looking marine animal. With hypnotic red-and-yellow colouration across its entire body, it definitely stands out on the sea floor. Its official name is *Metasepia pfefferi* and it can be found near Australia, as well as around the islands of the Pacific Ocean. It is not only highly toxic, but it is believed to be as poisonous as the blue-ringed octopus.

Cute but deadly

When we think of the dangers within the animal kingdom, we think of species like the lion, or a bear, maybe even a crocodile. We don't consider cute and adorable animals to pose a threat to us. Well, here are some cute animals that would send you to the afterlife with zero remorse.

The slow loris. When you see a slow loris you can't help but be awed by its cuteness, but if you do see one, remember to stay far away. Don't get tempted in by their big eyes, as they are the only poisonous primate. The pygmy slow loris produces a deadly toxin from glands located on its elbows — yes, that's right, its elbows! The primate will lick this area of its body to poison its teeth in case it needs to bite its prey. What's even more amazing is that the toxin is only activated when it is mixed with the loris's saliva; when it licks the toxin, the chemical reaction begins.

The hooded pitohui. With its distinctive green-and-gold appearance, the hooded pitohui looks like any other adorable bird, but it packs a nasty punch. Its feathers contain one of the most potent toxins known to science. A bird-watcher was attacked by one of these birds and it scratched his hands. He noticed the cuts hurt a lot more than they should have, and in an attempt to dull the pain he placed his fingers in his mouth, which made his tongue tingle and burn too. When the bird's features were examined more closely, it was found exactly why he had had such a reaction: there were batrachotoxins on the bird. These are extremely potent neurotoxins that can lead to paralysis, cardiac arrest and, worst-case scenario, death if administered in high doses.

Kooky koalas

Koalas are the dumbest mammals on Earth. If your favourite animal is the koala, then the next few facts are going to seem like koala blasphemy. The koala takes the award for dumbest mammal. They spend up to 20 hours a day sleeping because their main source of food is eucalyptus leaves, which provide them with very little energy.

A koala's diet is not great. Even though their diet almost entirely consists of eucalyptus plants, if you were to strip the eucalyptus leaves from the tree and put them on a plate in front of a koala, they wouldn't recognise them as food – they'd probably just stare at them.

Koalas don't get rain. Of all the koala facts I could share with you, this might just be my favourite. Koalas have been on the planet for approximately 25 million years, but to this day they do not understand the concept of rain. When it begins to rain, rather than seeking shelter, they will just sit there, confused about why they're getting wet, and they'll remain this way until it stops raining.

Koalas are more vicious than crocodiles. Don't let koalas' low IQ fool you; they know how to fight. Fun story: in 2006 a group of people broke into a zoo in Australia with the intention of stealing a koala, but they ended up leaving with a 1.2-metre-long, 40-kilogram crocodile, which they had to drag over a security fence, as that was easier than stealing a koala.

Sinister spiders

Spiders are becoming more abundant. Climate change is causing spiders to become not only more abundant but also larger. That's right, your worst nightmare is happening. A 2009 study showed that a warmer Arctic with earlier springs and a longer summer could make wolf spiders larger. And larger spiders have significantly more offspring, meaning spiders are becoming more abundant.

You are close to spiders all the time. This one might make you want to stay inside permanently. On average there are 50,000 spiders per acre in green areas. There will always be at least one spider less than a metre away from you, meaning you are always within arm's reach of a spider.

A spider's venom is not to be messed with. There's a spider that will cause your blood cells to burst because of the extremely rare protein found in the venom in its bite. If you were to be bitten by a spider in the genus *Loxosceles*, such as the feared brown recluse spider, the venom you were injected with would cause blackened skin at the point of impact.

Spiders 'drink' their prey. Now, I'm convinced spiders climbed out of the ninth circle of hell, and this fact might just prove it. Spiders don't just kill and eat their prey, they actually liquify it. They don't have any teeth and live on an entirely liquid diet. They possess a venom that is designed to break down cell walls. Some spiders have mandibles that eviscerate their prey and then shovel the leftovers into their mouths, where it is dissolved. Other species spit their venom onto their prey and wait for the unfortunate creature to liquify before they enjoy their 'delicious' drink.

Spider colonies are huge. Coming across one spider is bad enough, let alone thousands of them. The world is filled with spider colonies working together to build complex structures, as well as taking down prey several times their size. These colonies have the ability to house up to 50,000 spiders.

There is a spider that can eat birds. In my opinion, one of the scariest spiders in the world is the Goliath birdeater spider. Any spider that is classed as a 'birdeater' is the stuff of nightmares, but the Goliath birdeater spider's leg span can reach up to 28 centimetres and it has fangs more than six centimetres long. These measurements make this the largest species of spider.

Some spiders can jump. The idea that spiders can jump is pretty horrifying, but jumping spiders can jump 50 times their own body length.

Spiders are excellent listeners. Spiders have remarkable hearing, and it wasn't until recently that it was discovered spiders operate mostly via sight. However, researchers at Cornell University found that *Phidippus audax* (a species of jumping spider) can hear people up to three metres away, and very possibly even further. They hear through specialised hairs that detect particle movement.

A tarantula can defend itself. Generally tarantulas do not attack unless they are threatened. But when they are threatened, they will expel a cloud of poisonous hairs, known as urticating hairs, in an effort to defend themselves.

Some spiders can fly. Thought that it couldn't get any worse? I have two words for you: flying spiders. That's right. If you weren't arachnophobic before, you might be now. Flying spiders don't possess wings, but they do what is known as 'ballooning': they use threads of silk that they release into the wind to balloon their way through the air. They can use this method to travel hundreds of miles, even ending up on islands in the middle of the ocean. Looks like nowhere is safe.

Wild whales

Whales get too old and drown. This might be the saddest fact in the entire book. Whales are marine mammals that need to go to the surface every now and then to breathe, but when they reach a certain age, they become too physically weak to reach the surface, and so they drown.

Whales can hold their breath for an hour. Depending on the species, on average a whale can hold its breath for around 60 minutes. However, this does depend on its size, age and physical health.

The killer whale's menu is large and seemingly endless. Now I have to hand it to killer whales, they compete with dolphins for being the top menace of the ocean. For starters, almost nothing is too much for a killer whale – anyone and everyone is on the menu, from great whites to seals, to dolphins, to stingrays, to blue whales. Killer whales enjoy the privilege of being an apex predator.

Killer whales don't eat humans. You should be thankful that you are not a part of a killer whale's dietary needs. Humans have very little muscle and fat for their size, so we do not make a good, filling meal. This may seem like an insult, but you should be glad you have immunity from one of the most feared predators on the planet.

Killer whales do sometimes attack humans. The only time a killer whale will go after a human is if it has mistaken them for a seal, but when they realise their mistake they will stop the attack.

Killer whales throw their prey. Killer whales are brilliant hunters, but some of the ways they send their prey to the afterlife are just downright cruel. They have been documented jettisoning their next meal out of the water with their incredibly powerful tails. They can fling seals up to 24 metres into the air. They do this to significantly injure the animal even if it survives the fall. It also loosens the skin of their prey, making it easier to eat.

Killer whales will kill their own. When I say nothing in the ocean is safe, I mean nothing, even other killer whales. In fact, their young are at very high risk. Orcas have been known to assassinate other young orcas, with one intention: they will kill a child to have their shot at the grieving mother. This is very similar to mature lions.

Gargantuan gorillas

Gorillas are afraid of small creatures. We've all seen the films: *Planet of the Apes*, *King Kong* – you'd think gorillas aren't afraid of anything, but they are. The dreaded animals that gorillas fear the most are none other than chameleons and caterpillars. It's still unknown why they fear such small creatures, but it has been observed that even though baby mountain gorillas will follow every crawling thing out of interest, they will stop and give way to a chameleon or a caterpillar.

Gorillas are incredibly strong. To say that gorillas are strong might be stating the obvious, but just how strong are they? With each other they are quite gentle. However, when they pull out all the stops they have been known to bend metal bars to escape a cage or tear down banana trees like it's a regular old Wednesday, and their bite force is about double of that of a lion. Whereas a lion has a bite force of 650 psi (pounds per square inch), a gorilla's bite force is approximately 1,300 psi.

Gorillas don't like rain. Gorillas have a bad relationship with rain, so much so that if they get caught off-guard by a shower they will simply stay motionless and wait for it to stop, no matter how long it goes on for. If they know a cave is close by, they will go there for shelter, but otherwise they will just sit there. Orangutans, however, will occasionally use large leaves or branches to cover themselves.

Gorillas are kinda smelly. Gorillas, although very majestic creatures in the wild, are – how do I put this? – smelly. And the reason? They are constantly farting. Gorillas typically ingest 18–30 kilograms of vegetation every single day depending on whether they are male or female, and to be able to digest such a massive amount of food, their guts contain a large number of bacteria that cause them to fart almost constantly.

Gorillas are mostly vegetarian. You'd think that in order to become a 195-kilogram, physically strong animal, gorillas must have a very serious protein intake, but that isn't the case. Gorillas are mostly herbivorous, eating around 140 species of plants, and they need to consume between 18 and 30 kilograms of food per day.

Kicking kangaroos

Kangaroos have a secret. I wouldn't suggest getting this close to one, but let's say you were close enough to lift a kangaroo's tail off the ground – that would mean it wouldn't be able to hop. Kangaroos use their tails for balance when they are hopping, and if you were to lift their tail, they would have no balance and fall over.

Kangaroos are great fighters. The force that a kangaroo can exert is massive. The average human can punch with a force of 120–150 psi, while a kangaroo's punch generates a force of approximately 125 kilograms, and their kicks generate a massive 344 kilograms.

Kangaroos can really jump. Although kangaroos weigh 200 pounds, they can usually jump 1–2 metres high.

Kangaroos can send you to a watery grave. Whatever you do, never chase a kangaroo into water. If a kangaroo feels like it is in danger, it will attempt to lead its predator into water, up to the point where its arms are under the water. Then the kangaroo will hold the predator underwater until it either gives up or dies.

Kangaroos might also be the worst parents in the animal kingdom. When a kangaroo is being chased by a predator, in a last-ditch effort to get away, they have been known to drop their own children and flee, using them as a distraction or bait. The same behaviour has also been demonstrated by grey kangaroos.

Energetic emus

As we have previously discussed, humans once lost a war to the flightless bird known as the emu. *How?* you may ask. Well, let me explain how this hell pigeon got the one up on humans.

They travel in packs. Besides growing up to 6 feet tall, weighing 120 pounds, having the stamina of an Olympic athlete, running up to 30mph, and having an impressive vertical leap of 6.8 feet – *and* being strong swimmers – emus also flock in hordes of hundreds.

They are very intelligent. You might think that this bird is all brawn, no brains. However, this is not the case. In fact, emus gained a lot of respect during this war for their striking manoeuvrability as well as their tactical intelligence.

They outnumbered the humans. The sheer number of the emus was a massive disadvantage to humans. There were approximately 20,000 of these prehistoric-looking birds. After reading this, I think we should all have some sympathy for the soldiers that attempted to win this war.

They are sort of bulletproof. Over the course of the Great Emu War, the humans managed to confirm 986 emu kills using over 9,000 bullets to do so. That is approximately 10 bullets for every emu. Major Meredith, who was the Australian commander in the war, went on the record to say this about the birds: 'If we had a military division with the bullet-carrying capacity of these birds, it would face any army in the world. They can face machine guns with the invulnerability of tanks.' Not only are emus' feathers very thick but their organs also take up a very small area of their body, meaning you have to have perfect aim and knowledge of an emu's anatomy to take one down.

The best dads in nature

We've spoken a lot about bad parenting skills in the animal kingdom, but here are some more positive facts about good animal dads:

Marmosets. Once a male marmoset becomes a father, he takes the role very seriously, with the help of other family members. He takes on the responsibility for grooming, feeding and even giving his child piggyback rides, while the female marmosets step away after a few weeks. A primatologist at the University of Nebraska Zoo put this heavy involvement down to the male marmoset recognising the physical strain that is placed on the expectant mother.

Red foxes. When red foxes are young, their father will hunt every day for food. But after three months this comes to a stop, and instead of returning home with food, the father will bury it close to the family den in an attempt to teach his young how to forage.

Jacanas. Male jacana birds have been known to do all the hard work, from making nests to incubating the eggs and caring for the chicks once they are born. Female jacanas will 'get to know' another male once they have laid the eggs of another. Male jacanas are such caring, attentive creatures that they will even care for eggs fertilised by other males, and they will continue to stay with the nest after the females have left on their migration. Female jacanas help out by scaring away predators.

Arowanas. These fish carry their marble-like eggs in their mouths until they hatch. Once they hatch, the arowana fathers continue to keep hundreds of baby fish in their mouths for protection. The babies are let out to explore, and then the dad will seek out every offspring and suck them back into his mouth to keep them safe from predators.

Wolves. Wolves are known to the world as deadly apex predators, but they are monogamous, attentive to their young and extremely protective dads that stay with their mates for life. A female wolf will regurgitate meat to share with the litter, but the dad will provide whole pieces of fresh kill. As the young pup begins to grow, the father takes on a stern but playful role, gradually helping them to integrate into the pack.

Cockroaches. A creature you probably didn't expect to see on this list is the cockroach. They gather food for their young and they have been known to eat bird droppings to obtain nitrogen, which they then carry back to their young, as this is an essential nutrient for them (I do hope the young don't know where they're getting it from, though). Wood-feeding cockroaches are extremely meticulous and tidy parents, known to sweep entire nurseries, where they raise their young, to protect their families and ensure there is little to no risk of infection.

The best moms in nature

We've spoken about the best dads in nature, but what about the best moms? Let's talk about them.

Orangutans. The bond between a mother orangutan and her young is one of the strongest in nature. During the first two years of life, orangutan young rely on their mother entirely for food and transportation. The maternal orangutans don't check out after this; instead they stay with their young for six to seven years, teaching them valuable life lessons such as how to eat, how to build and how to stay safe when sleeping. As a thank you for all these important life lessons, orangutans visit their mothers until they reach the age of 15 or 16 – a very long time given that their average life expectancy is 27 years old.

Polar bears. Living in harsh conditions means mother polar bears must ensure their cubs stay with them for at least two years to be able to learn all the necessary survival skills. It all starts when an expectant mother keeps her young safe from the elements by digging into deep snow drifts to give birth; they usually do this anywhere between November and January in an attempt to keep the cubs warm and healthy using their body heat and milk. The cubs leave the den in March or April, as they need to get used to outside temperatures before they can learn the most important life skill: hunting.

Hamerkops. Hamerkops take their home DIY incredibly seriously. For approximately three to four months, these African birds will work relentlessly for hours every day to create a gigantic nest for their future young. The relationship between the hamerkop mother and father is very much built on teamwork. The male collects materials, while the female puts the intricate nest together. Once built, they will both cover the nest in mud and decorate it. The build is very impressive, measuring as large as 1.5 metres wide and 1.5 metres tall, and it can support the weight of an adult human. That shouldn't be a surprise though, as they contain as many as 8,000 pieces of assorted materials.

Giant Pacific octopuses. The giant Pacific octopus might just be the best mother of all. She will give birth to up to 74,000 eggs in a deep den or cave and take care of them for the next seven months, without leaving once, not even for food. This is a necessity to protect the babies from predators, but it is an act of self-sacrifice too. The mother octopus cannot survive without food and she will resort to living off the fats and proteins within her own body, eventually dying from self-cannibalisation.

Strawberry poison dart frogs. This frog is known to climb to great heights for its young. A mother will give birth on the Costa Rican rainforest floor and then, once the eggs hatch, she will individually carry each of her tadpoles to tiny pools of water, typically located in bromeliad leaves. Sometimes she has to carry them all the way up the tallest trees in the rainforest canopy. To keep her young fed until they metamorphose into froglets, she feeds each of her tadpoles one of her own unfertilised eggs.

Orca whales. If you like your sleep, you may not want to be a mother orca. There is quite literally no rest for orca mothers after their calves are born. They sacrifice sleep for the first month of their baby's life, but not by choice. Newborn killer whales don't sleep for the first month of their lives. Instead, they keep on swimming, helping them not only to avoid predators but also to build up crucial fat reserve and muscle. Some orca mothers are even known to stay with their pod for their entire lives, meaning the mother and child always stay together. Tell me that isn't wholesome.

Taita African caecilian. Many mothers in the animal kingdom would, as the saying goes, give the skin off their own back for their young if they could. Well, for the Taita African caecilian this isn't just a saying – they literally do this. Once the mum's eggs have hatched, she will grow an extra, nutritious layer of skin for her children to eat. This extra skin will grow back every three days until her young become more independent and find their own food source that isn't, well, their own mother.

Alligators. The alligator is one of the animals that could have you knocking on heaven's door the quickest, but it's also a massive softy when it comes to parenthood. Alligator mothers are extremely caring. Once their eggs hatch and they have officially brought new life into the world, the mum will put all the babies into her jaws and carry them safely to the water. Alligators ensure their children stay with them for at least two years as, unfortunately, 80 per cent of baby alligators fall victim to predators. The mother does everything she can to protect them for this period of time, so although the majority of the young die, the mother does give parenthood a good old college try, which is why I think they're deserving of a place on this list.

Hornbills. Mother hornbills do not mess around when it comes to the safety and protection of their young. Their nests are among the safest – the mother will build it inside the hollow part of a tree and then, for extra protection, when it's time to lay and incubate the eggs she will seal herself and her future babies inside using fruit and mud, leaving a small enough opening for the father to sneak food through to her.

Party animals

I won't beat around the bush with this one: this is how different species of animals get high.

Wallabies have a poppy addiction. Let's talk about wallabies. Their addiction was first discovered by poppy farmers in Australia. They were growing poppies for the pharmaceutical industry, but they began noticing strangely damaged crops on their land. The poppy fields were filled with massive circular marks, and when the farmers saw this, they immediately thought ET's mothership had landed – but that isn't right. It appeared that wallabies had been breaking into the fields to eat a large amount of poppies, which would have made them very high, to the point that they could only hop in circles, over and over again. And this was not a one-time thing. Once the wallabies got a taste of the high, they itched for it again and again and caused even more damage.

Black lemurs get high off poison. Black lemurs quite literally risk it all for a little high. You see, they have been known to gnaw the heads off giant millipedes, but not for food, because millipedes are actually poisonous. Once their head is ripped off, they excrete a number of defensive toxins, including cyanide. It's no surprise that if the lemur ingests them, they will get hurt, but they have found out that if they rub the toxins on their bodies, they will get high. I haven't a clue which black lemur came to this realisation, but it is hilarious to me. These chemicals, once spread on the black lemur's body, act as a narcotic, so if a lemur finds itself bored or even stressed, it's time to go out and find a millipede.

Horses have a secret addiction too. Horses don't know when to stop. Locoweeds are a group of approximately 20 types of weed that live in the western USA. They grow throughout the winter and have become an 'attractive' food for nearby horses. It has been found that once the horses have tasted the weed a couple of times, they come back seasonally, in the summer, spring and autumn. The horses become severely addicted, and when I say 'severely', I mean it, because locoweed is poisonous. The horses are literally eating themselves to death on locoweed over the course of a few years. In certain parts of the USA this has become such a problem that there are whole sites dedicated to detoxing horses from locoweed.

Birds can make their own drugs. Some bird species are the *Breaking Bad* stars of the animal kingdom. That's right, birds can essentially 'cook up' new compounds. Species such as jays, ravens, blackbirds and parrots have been observed actively squashing ants and pushing them into their plumage. Once the birds are covered in dead ants, they will spin around for up to half an hour before shaking them off. It was originally believed the birds did this to use the formic acid the ants secreted in order to clean off any parasites they may have picked up – that was until domesticated magpies were seen rolling their bugs in tobacco ash before placing them on their bodies. Essentially, these different compounds get them hooked.

Animals can get high off their own bodies. This one is a bit more of a desperate attempt to get high. In the absence of a physical substance that can get them high, some species of birds and rodents will search for their own physiological high in the form of 'self-drugging', by banging their own heart repeatedly. Scientists have said they aren't entirely sure whether they do this to try to dull other pain or whether it releases endorphins that make the animal 'feel good'.

Brown bears will do anything for their next high. It turns out bears have their own way of getting high. Specifically, brown bears at the Kronotsky Nature Reserve in the far east of Russia are apparently addicted to jet fuel. A photographer spent seven months documenting a community of bears who would play with discarded/empty barrels, sniffing gasoline and kerosene and subsequently getting high off the fumes. It has gotten to the point where they will stalk helicopters for their next hit; they will wait patiently for the fuel to leak onto the soil when the helicopters land and take off.

Elephants learn about drugs from a young age. Elephant parents can be a bad influence. I know we previously spoke about them being wholesome, but they do enjoy the odd trip as well. Elephant groups have been known to gather around the iboga plant, an evergreen shrub found in the rainforest and native to Central Africa, and a powerful hallucinogenic. The elephants will eat the iboga plant and, to put it bluntly, get completely baked. It doesn't stop there, however, as elephants are generally led by their oldest and most experienced members. This is because they have a teaching society. The young in particular look up to the older members to learn essential future skills, and I suppose one of those skills is how to get completely spaced out.

Ants can get very protective over their stash. Similar to humans, if someone tries to take an ant stash that isn't theirs, the ants get very aggressive. Acacia trees have been known to be protected by herds of ants, but why is that? Because from that tree comes sugary syrup. At first glance you might think the syrup is just nutritional, but scientists recently found out that it is also very addictive. The ants, with no shame, will feed this addiction to their heart's content, and if any animal attempts to threaten the tree – even larger animals – they will attack.

Birds know how to ferment their next high. Once again we return to the avid high-seekers that are birds. It appears all kinds of birds enjoy the buzz that comes from feeding on fruit that has fallen to the ground and been left to ferment, and just like humans should never drive under the influence, birds should never fly drunk. Intoxicated birds often lose the ability to orientate themselves, control their speed and even stop. And that's not the only danger: because many birds are so physically small, it's very easy for them to die from an overdose. Thankfully, species such as the waxwing have larger livers, which gives them a slightly higher tolerance to fermented berries.

Being high might make jaguars better hunters.
Let's talk about the fearsome big cat of the Amazon rainforest, the jaguar. Jaguars have been known to chew the intoxicating and nauseating bark, leaves and vines of the yage plant. The consumption of this plant has been observed to cause pupillary dilation and it is theorised that jaguars use it in a quest to tighten their sensory perception to make them better hunters. Essentially, these are the sport-enhancing drugs of the animal kingdom.

Dolphins have their own secret to getting high. Most people's favourite ocean animal is the dolphin for their absolute elegance, but now I'm going to completely ruin your perception of them by telling you about their recreational drug use. Yes, you read that right, dolphins actually get high off a neurotoxin that is released from pufferfish. In small amounts this toxicity has a narcotic effect, and so they carefully chew on and then pass the pufferfish between them.

CHAPTER 8:

FOOD

Food is something
we all consume every
single day, but have
you ever thought about
the specific ingredients
within food, or where
the food you eat
actually comes from?
Let's just say if you
love your food, you will
not love this chapter.
I wish you luck before
you begin.

General facts

The origins of hot chocolate. Hot chocolate, an almost universally enjoyed beverage, has been around for a very long time, most likely longer than you think. In fact, the Mayan and Aztec civilisations were the first cultures known to make hot chocolate. It was initially used for religious ceremonies, including weddings.

Honey is not what you think it is. Honey is basically bee vomit. Bees have different roles, and one of the most important is forager bee. These bees collect nectar from flowering plants. However, they can't carry all these foraged goods in a backpack; the foragers will drink the nectar and keep it in their 'honey stomach'. When they return to the hive, they will regurgitate the nectar into the honey stomach of the processor bee, which is placed near the entrance of the hive, and the processor bee will then regurgitate it into the hive, allowing it to ripen.

Seasoning too much can get you high. The vast majority of hallucinogens are banned, but you might not realise that there is one hallucinogen that might be in your diet. Nutmeg is technically a hallucinogen: a compound that can cause hallucinations. The compounds in nutmeg are myristicin and safrole, both of which are used in various illegal synthetic drugs.

Peanut butter can be explosive. In the wrong hands, the peanuts you keep in your cupboard could go from being a healthy snack to deadly dynamite. I'm not joking. Peanuts contain an oil known as glycerol, which is used to create nitroglycerine, a key ingredient in dynamite.

The British didn't invent teabags. Now, British people are known around the world for their tea obsession, so you'd be forgiven for thinking that the teabag was invented in Britain, but in fact teabags were invented by an American man by the name of Thomas Sullivan, who revolutionised this drink. He sent samples of the product in silk bags, which even to his surprise people began to put in teapots, and thus teabags came into existence. Who knew that such a delicious drink was a happy accident?

You can buy the world's most expensive ice-cream sundae in New York. We all love an ice-cream sundae, but just how much would you be prepared to pay for one? Well, I guarantee most of you wouldn't want to pay as much as the Golden Opulence Sundae at Serendipity3 in New York City costs. It contains Tahitian vanilla cream topped with 23-carat gold leaf, almonds and caviar, along with a sugar-encrusted orchid. You'll need a lot of cash and also some spare time on your hands if you want to give it a go, because it takes up to eight hours to make and comes in a $350 Baccarat crystal goblet with an 18-carat gold spoon. The whole thing will set you back $1,000 and needs to be ordered 48 hours in advance.

Pretzels were the romantic food of the past. During the seventeenth century, pretzels were used to symbolise undying love, so much so that in 1614 a Swiss royal couple used a pretzel in their wedding to seal the bond. Many historians believe this is where the saying 'tying the knot' came from.

Ranch dressing is just suncream. Did you know that there's an unexpected ingredient in ranch salad dressing? Ranch dressing contains titanium dioxide, which is actually used in sunscreen to give it the bright white colour we're all familiar with.

Ketchup used to be a popular medicine. Ketchup wasn't always just a delicious dip for your chips. During the 1830s ketchup was said to have medicinal properties. People believed it could cure diarrhoea, indigestion, jaundice and rheumatism and so it was heavily consumed.

White chocolate isn't actually chocolate. Which is better: milk, plain or white chocolate? Well, I have some difficult news for white chocolate lovers. In fact, white chocolate isn't really chocolate at all. It doesn't contain dark chocolate cacao solids, which means it cannot be classed as real chocolate.

Carrots have an interesting side effect. As children, we were always told to eat our carrots as they can help improve our night vision. That's just a myth, but they can turn your skin orange. Multiple studies have found that eating an abundance of carrots can gradually turn your skin an orange-yellow colour; this is known as carotenemia and it is physically harmless. Mentally, however, not so much, as every time you look in a mirror you will feel like an Oompa Loompa.

The Ancient Greeks had tree-flavoured chewing gum.
What would you prefer to chew on: chewing gum or birch bark? Well, if you lived approximately 9,000 years ago in Europe, you would have had access to a form of gum, but it would have been birch bark. If you lived in ancient Greece, you would have chewed mastic gum, which was made from the resin of the mastic tree. It contained antiseptic properties and was believed to maintain oral health.

You'll never guess who invented candy floss.
Candy floss contains a lot of sugar, so you would think the last person who would have come up with it would be a dentist. But what if I told you that is exactly the case? In 1897 a dentist partnered with a confectioner and together they created candy floss, which was originally called 'fairy floss'. Decades later, in 1921, another dentist created a similar fairy floss machine and called it 'cotton candy', which caught on a lot more than fairy floss.

Lollipops have been around for thousands of years.
There is a belief among historians that cavemen invented lollipops by collecting honey from beehives with a stick.

The first food eaten by an American in space was applesauce. In 1962 after successfully reaching orbit in the Mercury Friendship 7 spacecraft, American astronaut John Glenn ate applesauce from a tube.

The first meal eaten in space had two courses.
John Glenn was not the first person to eat in space. That honour goes to Yuri Alekseyevich Gagarin when he orbited Earth on board Vostok 1 in April 1961. He ate beef and liver paste squeezed from a tube, followed by chocolate sauce for dessert.

Chocolate chip cookies were invented by accident.
You would think that something as completely perfect as a chocolate chip cookie would have been created out of sheer precision and determination, but this is not true. The creation of the legendary chocolate chip cookie was an accident. Some believe that someone called Ruth Wakefield unexpectedly ran out of nuts for ice-cream cookies and instead used chunks of chocolate. The other theory is that chocolate chunks fell into an industrial mixer. However, these are both rumours and neither is confirmed.

We have a queen to thank for Margherita pizza.
Margherita pizza was named after a queen. In 1889 King Umberto I and Queen Margherita visited Naples. While they were there they got bored of fancy food and requested pizza, which at the time was a food for the poor. The queen was served pizza mozzarella, which was topped with soft white cheese, tomatoes and basil. She loved it so much that from then on it was known as the Margherita pizza.

Bananas are technically radioactive. This is due to the fact that they are so rich in potassium. Granted, a human contains more potassium than a banana, which means that we are even more radioactive.

We have cyanide in our food. Lima beans and cyanide are two things you would hope not to see together in the same sentence, but actually raw lima beans contain a large amount of cyanide, which is lethal to humans. However, don't get too concerned: as long as the beans are thoroughly cooked, they are completely safe to eat.

Watermelon is not a fruit. Watermelon is the official vegetable of Oklahoma. That's right, the watermelon is part of the *Cucurbitaceae* family, which also contains cucumbers and pumpkins, and so some people think it must be a vegetable. However, if you were to ask a botanist, they would say that this summer produce is a fruit.

Fruits eat us back. We eat fruit all the time, but what if I told you that there is a certain fruit that eats you back? Pineapple contains an enzyme known as bromelain that breaks down proteins, so next time you notice that tingly or burning sensation in your mouth after eating pineapple, know that this is because the pineapple you just consumed is breaking down some of your proteins and eating you back.

You can taste foods through your feet. If you were to put your feet in a bag of garlic and move them around, you would be able to taste them. This isn't because you have special taste buds in your feet, but because the molecule allicin, which is responsible for the very specific garlic scent, can penetrate the skin on your feet, enter your bloodstream and travel to your nose and mouth, causing you to taste garlic.

You could turn peanut butter into diamonds. If you have a jar of peanut butter in your home, you could turn it into diamonds. As we know, diamonds are formed when carbon atoms are put under high temperature and pressure, so under the right conditions peanut butter – which is relatively high in carbon – could form diamonds. Granted, the process is slow and quite messy: a scientist called Frost at the Bayerisches Geoinstitut in Germany attempted to create diamonds from carbon-rich peanut butter, but a lot of hydrogen was released, which destroyed the experiment. He says this only happened 'after it had been converted to diamond'.

A mushroom is your ancestor. What if I told you that mushrooms are more closely related to humans than to plants? Animals and fungi surprisingly share a common ancestor. They separated from plants roughly a billion years ago, and it was after this that animals and fungi separated, making them more closely related to each other than to plants.

Mountain Dew was invented as a mixer. Mountain Dew wasn't originally made to be a pop; rather it was invented as a mixer for whiskey. It was created in the Smoky Mountains in Tennessee by brothers Barney and Ally Hartman. The name 'Mountain Dew' was originally a nickname for moonshine, and the brothers decided to give their mixer this name as they joked that it tasted like moonshine once it was mixed with liquor. There was, however, a slight difference between Mountain Dew then and the drink we know and love today. It used to be a clear, caffeine-free lemon-and-lime beverage that has more similarities with Sprite than today's Mountain Dew.

Red seaweed is a popular ingredient. You may not know this but seaweed is used in many of the dairy products we know and love. Yogurt, soured cream, ice cream and cottage cheese are just some of these products. Red seaweed contains a natural plant fibre known as carrageenan that can be found in dairy products; it is used for its thickening and stabilising properties.

Horrifying food facts

Peanut butter comes with a side of insects. A typical jar of peanut butter is allowed to contain one or more rodent hairs. A jar would need to contain an average of 30 or more insect fragments per 100 grams before it is considered unsanitary enough to pose a health hazard to consumers.

You will never look at oysters the same again. Raw oysters are still alive when you eat them. They are alive because they go bad very quickly, which means restaurants serve them as fresh as they can possibly be. Once they die, the bacteria makes them no longer safe to eat.

The natural flavouring in vanilla ice cream has a strange origin. Let me ask you something, what is your favourite flavour of ice cream? Mint choc chip, chocolate, strawberry – how about vanilla? Well, if your answer is vanilla, you should probably know that a number of your favourite vanilla-flavoured treats are made with an ingredient called castoreum. This is referred to as 'natural flavouring' on ingredient labels, but have you stopped to think about where it comes from? Probably not, right? Well, it comes from the castor sac scent glands of beavers, which are actually located near their anuses.

Canned mushrooms contain a secret surprise. For some reason, animals and animal parts seem to find their way into our food. We have spoken about peanut butter, and the same goes for canned mushrooms, which may contain maggots. Once again, this is according to US Food and Drug Administration regulations. 'Canned mushrooms are allowed to contain over 20 or more maggots of any size per 100 grams of drained mushrooms and proportionate liquid' before they are considered to be unnatural or defective.

Hot dogs contain traces of ... never mind. Let's take a minute to talk about hot dogs. This one hurts even me. In 2015 a company called Clear Labs released serious allegations surrounding hot dogs, saying that 2 per cent of the hot dogs they tested contained traces of human DNA. Now thankfully the headlines about this were proven to be misleading, but that doesn't mean hot dogs are completely out of the woods yet. In fact, the tested products did show that they contained traces of human hair, skin and nails. What's even worse is that 10 per cent of the tested hot dogs that were branded 'vegetarian' contained real meat.

There is a secret to the colour of jellybeans. Jellybeans and other glazed sweets are commonly coated in insect secretions. Yes, you read that one right. Certain sweets contain shellac, a processed and hardened resin that is secreted by a female bug called *Kerria lacca* that lives in India and Thailand. Food companies dissolve these hardened flakes in ethanol and then use this as a brush-on colourant and food glaze for sweets. If you want to make sure your sweets are shellac-free, just remember that it is sometimes described as 'confectioner's glaze' or 'food additive number E904' on food labels.

There are bugs in our drinks too. If you look at a food label and it reads 'carmine' or 'natural red 4', this essentially means red food colouring, but that colouring is derived from ground and boiled cochineal bugs – a type of beetle. Starbucks used cochineal extract until 2012, when it got out to the public that this ingredient was in drinks like their Strawberries & Cream Frappuccino Blended Beverage. Other foods that use this colouring include ketchup, syrup, artificial crab meat, ice cream, yogurt and red velvet cake.

You will never look at gummy sweets the same way again. It's almost impossible to eat gummy sweets because, let's be honest, they look way too cute. One of the main ingredients in gummy sweets is gelatin. This is a virtually colourless and tasteless water-soluble protein that comes from collagen. So what's wrong with that? As it turns out, collagen is actually extracted from the skin, bones and tissues of animals, generally pigs and cattle. This changes everything for me.

There are wasp carcasses in our fruit. This might sound strange, but did you know that figs are not a fruit? They are actually flowers that are inverted and have bloomed internally, and on top of that they typically have at least one dead wasp trapped inside them. Humans only eat female figs, because wasps are known to lay their larvae inside male figs. The wasp then proceeds to die inside the fig, having faith that the babies will burrow out and continue the cycle. However, like many things, this is not a perfect process, and the wasp can get the wrong fig every now and then. Thankfully, just in case this happens, figs have a specific enzyme known as ficin that breaks down the wasp carcass and transforms it into a protein. Granted, if you were to eat a fig, the wasp remains would be unrecognisable and incredibly small, but now you know that they might be there.

CHAPTER 9:

BONUS FACTS

This chapter is full of unlikely, near-impossible scenarios — and the facts that just might save you from them. Read on to find out how you could live to tell the tale if you ever find yourself in one of these survival situations.

Facts that could save your life one day

General facts

What not to do in an aeroplane crash. If your aeroplane crashes into the water, don't inflate your life vest until after you get out, otherwise you could get trapped inside the plane as the water levels rise.

The essential rules for survival come in threes. You should always remember these rules when it comes to survival: you can survive for three minutes without air, three hours without shelter, three days without water and three weeks without food.

Follow a solo service dog. If a service dog ever approaches you without their owner, the best thing you can do is follow them, and quickly – they might be leading you back to their owner who is in trouble, and you could save their life.

There is an international number for 'help'. If you are in a foreign country and need to call for help, you might not know the emergency number in that area. If in doubt, call 112. This is the international emergency number and will automatically connect you to the nearest helpline.

Avoid square waves if you're in the sea. If you're ever swimming in the sea and notice square waves beginning to appear, you need to calmly exit the water as quickly as possible. Real danger lurks beneath those waves: immensely strong currents that will pull you under and kill you in an instant. These dangerous currents are formed when two wave systems meet. They are so deadly that a study in 2004 showed that a larger percentage of ship accidents occur in cross-sea states.

Always hold your nose when jumping into water.
Staying with water, if you are ever about to jump into a river or lake, it's always best to hold your nose. This acts as protection from any amoebas lurking in the water that will crawl up your nose cavity upon impact.

Choose green coconuts over brown coconuts. If you ever find yourself in a survival situation, to be safe it is best to drink coconut water from green coconuts only. These are the youngest and thus have the purest and safest water. Brown coconuts are fully matured and thus contain oils that cause dehydration.

Beware if you notice a fishy smell in your home.
If your house smells like fish for no apparent reason, nine times out of ten it means that somewhere in your house there is an electrical fire. When electrical parts begin to overheat, they release a fishy odour.

Step, don't jump, out of a moving vehicle. If you're ever in a situation where you need to escape from a moving vehicle, you should definitely not just jump straight out – real life is not like the movies. Instead, you should put one foot down and take a step. This method will actually significantly reduce your speed and dramatically increase your chances of survival.

What to do if you have been kidnapped. On the subject of car-related survival situations, if you are ever stuffed into the back of a car, try to stay calm – there is a lot of meddling you can do in the boot. You could try to disconnect the brake light wires, so if the driver passes a police officer, they will get pulled over. Take this as your moment to kick the roof of the boot and let them know you're there.

When you should and shouldn't swerve. When an animal steps into the road, it's human instinct to swerve and try not to hit the poor creature. However, I do have a minor adjustment to make to that thought process. If, for example, a deer runs across the road, it is better to hit it than to swerve, as your chances of survival if you hit the deer are significantly higher than if you swerve into a ditch. However, if a moose comes into the middle of the road, it's better to swerve and run into the ditch; hitting a moose is like running into a brick wall.

Eating snow can be deadly. In any survival situation, no matter how thirsty you become, one thing you should never do is eat large amounts of snow. Having too much cool ice in your stomach has a high chance of causing hypothermia, which can be fatal. The best option is to melt the ice first and then drink it.

Kneel down if you're about to get struck by lightning. If you're enjoying a casual day out and suddenly someone points out that your hair is standing up like it's static, I don't mean to panic you, but you are about to be struck by lightning. When electric storms are strong enough to make your hair stand up, it means you are in imminent danger. Immediately drop to your knees and bend forwards, without lying flat on the ground. Wet ground is a very good conductor of electricity.

Always bunny hop around electricity. If a power line ever falls next to you, do not walk or run away from it. To avoid electrocution and even death, you should put your feet together and bunny hop to get away from the area safely. This will keep the electricity from travelling up one of your legs and down the other, and as a result it will stop you from getting shocked by several thousand volts.

Vodka can save lives. If you ever wind up in a situation where you have ingested windshield wiper fluid or antifreeze, you need to grab a bottle of liquid courage and drink it. That's right, consuming large amounts of vodka will actually prevent the wiper fluid or antifreeze from shredding your kidneys, giving you time to get to the hospital.

A random gas smell in your house. If you ever wake up to the smell of gas, do not turn on any lights. There is a chance that one spark from the light switch could blow up your entire house.

Elevators can tell you the quickest exit. If you ever find yourself in an emergency in a multi-storey building, look at the main panel in the elevator. If you see a floor number with a star next to it, that indicates a floor with an emergency exit. Then proceed to take the stairs to that floor.

Always look after your drink. If you're ever out or at a party and your drink suddenly begins to taste salty, don't keep drinking it, go and tell someone – a friend or a person who works at the establishment you're in. Rohypnol is reported to have a slightly salty taste. This is a drug that causes blackouts and memory loss from the time it is ingested.

Spitting can help you survive an avalanche. If you're ever buried inside an avalanche, it can be very difficult to know which way is up and you will feel very disorientated. The best thing you can do is make an air pocket around your face with your hands and spit. Your saliva will follow gravity and you must then simply dig in the opposite direction.

You can quickly work out if you're being followed. If you're ever in a situation where you believe you're being followed by another driver and you want to make sure, take four right turns. This will take you in a complete circle. If the same driver is still behind you, this means there's a high chance you are indeed being followed. Don't alert them to the fact that you know they're following you and instead drive to a police station. Do not be tempted to drive home.

Don't give in to temptation. If you are ever out and about and see money falling from the sky, don't run towards it (as tempting as it might seem); instead, run away immediately. This is because terrorists can drop money as a tactic to get a large number of unsuspecting people into one area.

Different coloured beach flags have different meanings. If I were to ask you about beach flags and their meanings, could you tell me all of them? Probably not, because usually we're only told about the big red one that means 'hazard' or 'rough conditions'. In actuality, there are many different flags with many different colours. Here are their meanings so you can keep yourself safe. If there is a double red flag, one on top of another, this means the water is closed to the public. A yellow flag means there is a medium hazard, potentially a light surf or currents that could pose a threat. A green flag depicts a low hazard, meaning relatively calm conditions. Finally, there's the purple flag, which tells you there are marine pests like jellyfish, stingrays or dangerous fish in the water. These are worldwide signs supported by the International Life Saving Federation.

You can survive quicksand by doing the backstroke.
Getting stuck in quicksand is one of those nightmare
situations, but if it happens to you, here's what you
should do. Immediately get rid of any belongings you
have on you to make yourself lighter. If you are waist
deep, get into a floating position on your back, as this
will help you get your feet back towards the surface.
Gradually move towards solid ground, using methods
like the backstroke; do this slowly and calmly while
continuously bringing your feet closer to the surface.
Remember, for every few centimetres you raise your feet,
allow a moment to pass before moving again to ensure
that the sand has filled in the pocket where your feet
previously were. This technique takes some time. During
the whole process, make sure you are breathing deeply;
this will keep you calm and help with your buoyancy.

Don't mix chemicals. Whatever you do, do not mix bleach and ammonia. When mixed, this combination can actually make a poisonous gas – a toxic compound known as chloramine vapour, which can very easily form poisonous hydrazine.

Call for rescue using a pattern. If you are ever buried under rubble – for example, after a building collapse – and are unable to get out, your first instinct might be to yell, but this will waste your energy, tire you out and make you lose your voice. Try and find something to tap on and tap it in intervals of three. Human beings are great at noticing patterns, and rescuers at the scene will move towards that sound. Once you can tell that they're within hearing distance, then you can start yelling to confirm your location to them.

Animal facts to save your life

We have spoken about general facts to save your life, but what if you are fighting against members of the animal kingdom? Here is what you need to do if you are being approached or attacked by different animals.

Wolves. Being out in the wild and seeing a pack of wolves staring you down would easily make the list of things that would make you want to run away and scream, but I highly encourage you not to do that. Instead, stand your ground against a wolf pack. You see, wolves will only attack you if they are able to intimidate you into running in the opposite direction.

Bears. What about a bear? With some you should go on the attack; with others you need to play dead. Here's a safety rhyme about bears of all colours: 'If it's black, fight back. If it's brown, lay down. If it's white, goodnight.' Generally speaking, a good rule to follow is that if a bear begins to approach you, never try to run away, because even Usain Bolt, the fastest man alive, could not outrun a bear. Also, avoid eye contact.

Cougars. A video of a cougar getting angry and approaching a hiker with less than pure intentions went viral on the internet, and no surprise, because these might be one of the scariest wild animals to come face to face with. However, there are some things you can do to massively increase your survival chances. Always maintain eye contact – unlike with a bear, this is crucial, and when I say 'eye contact', I mean do not even for a second take your eye off the animal. As you maintain eye contact, slowly back away. On top of this, be loud – yell at it, swear at it, whatever you have to do to tell that animal you are not prey.

Mountain gorillas. Coming across an angry mountain gorilla seems like a far-fetched idea, but I would prefer to be overprepared than underprepared. Unlike a lot of the animals I have mentioned, if you start acting bigger and trying to intimidate them, the gorilla will humble you into the ground. The best thing to do is to go into a submissive position, even getting on the ground and making yourself limp, in an attempt to show the walking triceps workout that you mean it no harm. Three things not to do: run away, make direct eye contact or show your teeth.

Lions. Let's talk about the king of the jungle, the lion. Although they originate from Africa, there have over the years been reports of lion attacks in zoos in other parts of the world. Now, although this sounds crazy, if one were to attack you, you should muster all your might and fight it. Act and look as big as you can, make sure it knows you are not an easy target that will just let it make you an all-you-can-eat buffet. You want the lion to see you as strong, never weak, and they can also sense fear, so if you run, they will take you to be easy prey. One thing you should never do around a lion is play dead or curl into the foetal position.

Alligators. If an alligator grabs you, shove your finger in its nose. This breaks the airway seal, allowing water to flush in.

While we're on the topic of alligators, if an alligator feels annoyed enough to come for you on land, contrary to popular belief, you should never run in a zigzag line. They are not as stupid as many believe and will catch you. Just run in a straight line, and run fast, keeping in mind that they can run up to 35mph.

Sharks. Going from land to sea, we have one of the most feared creatures on the planet, the shark. Now, to protect yourself you are advised not to use your bare hands or feet, but rather to use whatever weapons you can find. However, I'm betting the pockets of your swimming trunks aren't that deep, so let's assume you don't have anything on you. Focus your punches, pokes and kicks on the delicate parts of the shark, including its eyes and gills. The same applies if the shark actually manages to get you inside its mouth. There are sensitive parts that are exposed on a shark, so muster any calmness you have left and go to town.

Octopuses. If you're ever in the ocean and get grabbed by an octopus, do not try to prune it off you. Let's be honest, they have eight tentacles (or, scientifically speaking, arms) – you aren't going to win that fight. The key to survival in this situation is to get the octopus off its anchor point, which will most likely be a rock or a pipe. If you knock the octopus off, it will not be able to pull you down and thus will be forced to let you go.

Bees and wasps. If you ever accidentally do the unthinkable and disturb a beehive or a wasp's nest, my one piece of advice would be *not* to run for the water. For some reason, that is our first thought, but the insects will just wait for you to resurface and continue to sting you. Your best bet is to run as fast and as far as you can and do not stop; eventually the bees or wasps will stop following you.

Facts that will change your perception of time

This section is completely mind-boggling and full of facts that will change the way you think about, well, everything.

Sharks are older than the rings of Saturn. The distinctive rings that surround the massive celestial body Saturn only formed approximately 10–100 million years ago. Surely very little in the world we know today can have existed for that long, but Saturn's rings are still relatively young compared to the 450-million-year existence of sharks.

Sharks are also older than trees. The first actual tree appeared 65 million years after sharks did, in the Devonian period.

The high five has only been around since the 1970s. The high five is a gesture of friendship and appreciation that you might think has been around forever, but it was only on 2 October 1977 that the first real high five is considered to have taken place. During a historic game of baseball, Dusty Baker hit his thirtieth home run of the season for the LA Dodgers. He rounded the bases one by one and a rookie by the name of Glenn Burke met him at the final plate, raising his arm into the air and slapping Baker's hand. Thus the high five was created.

Elon Musk's wealth is absurd. Elon Musk is famed for being one of the richest men in the world, but it's difficult to fathom just how much cash he has. Let's put it this way – if you had been given $10,000 every day since the pyramids of Egypt were constructed 4,500 years ago, you would still only have roughly 6 per cent of what Elon has. Those $10,000 a day would equate to roughly $16.4 billion, and he is currently sitting at $274.3 billion.

A billion is mind-bogglingly bigger than a million. A million and a billion both sound like big numbers, but it's easy to forget just how far apart these two numbers are. Try this: a million seconds ago was a little over a week ago, whereas a billion seconds ago was in the year 1990.

You shouldn't try to counting to a billion. Another way of picturing the scale of these two numbers is this. If you were to count to a million at the approximate rate of one number per second, it would take you 11 days. However, if you were to count to a billion at the same rate, it would take you 32 years. I'm not sure even MrBeast would attempt this one. What if you were to count to a trillion, though? That would take you 31,709 years.

Dinosaurs could have found dinosaur fossils.
Dinosaurs lived on the planet for such a long time compared to humans that we are just a speck on the timeline compared to them. To put it into perspective, dinosaur fossils existed while dinosaurs were still alive.

Grass is younger than the dinosaurs. Yes, grass. Grass only began to flourish on earth 66 million years ago, just before the asteroid caused the extinction of the dinosaurs 65 million years ago. This means dinosaurs were able to enjoy grass for just 1 million years of their 252 million years of existence.

George Washington didn't know dinosaurs existed.
George Washington died in 1799, but humans didn't prove the existence of dinosaurs until 1841, which means that this US president lived without knowing dinosaurs existed.

The planet has a drastically increasing human population. If you are older than 45, then the population of the world has doubled in your lifetime. For reference, in 1978 the population of the earth was approximately 4 billion. In 2023, 45 years later, the population as of writing is 8,035,199,255.

Humans are an incredibly young species. Humans have only existed for 0.004 per cent of earth's history.

You don't truly know how old you are. Let me ask you something – how old are you? Right now, reading this book? What if I told you that you are wrong? Well, kind of. Every atom in your body is billions of years old. Hydrogen, which is the most common element in the universe and a major component of your body, was produced in the universe 13.7 billion years ago.

There are a lot of us on the planet right now. Six per cent of all humans to have ever existed in the entire history of humanity exist right now.

Acknowledgements

I would like to acknowledge several people in my life without whom I would not be where I am today. Firstly, my incredible parents. Mum, Dad, thank you for always pushing me and always being supportive in my dreams of pursuing a career online. There aren't many parents who would put up with the last almost decade of constant filming, but you both did. You helped me through university, you bought me my first camera. I dedicate a lot of my success to you.

To my wonderful partner, Chloe. The person by my side every single day pushing me to be the best version of myself, motivating and encouraging me! I love you and thank you for everything you have ever done for me.

To my management, Alpha Talent. You have done so much for my career over the past two years of working together. Thank you, Jake and Nadia, for making this all possible.

I want to thank everyone at Ebury for allowing me to create this book. Without your advice, guidance and belief in this project it would not be possible.

About the author

Matthew Carter, known online as MjcMatthew, has accumulated 5 million followers across his social media platforms. After receiving a BSc in Environmental Earth Science and an MSc in Forensic Science, he turned his attention to educating the online world about the craziest, least well-known, most mind-boggling facts that have ever existed.